Full
Esteem
Ahead

"I began to understand that
self-esteem isn't everything;
it's just that there's nothing
without it."

GLORIA STEINEM, 1992

FULL ESTEEM AHEAD

Keys to Strong Personal Values
and
Positive Self-Esteem

By

Rob Solomon, M.A., L.P.C.

Edited by

Paula J. Hunter

Kincaid
HOUSE

Book design, cover design and illustration by John Benson, Newport Beach, California.

Printed and bound in the United States of America.

Library of Congress Cataloging-in-Publication Data

Solomon, Rob, 1954-
Full Esteem Ahead : keys to strong personal values and positive
    self-esteem / Rob Solomon ; edited by Paula J. Hunter.
        p.   cm.
    Includes bibliographical references.
    ISBN 0-943793-33-5
    1. Self-respect.   2. Values.   I. Hunter, Paula J.   II. Title
BF697.5.S46S65   1992
158'.1--dc20   92-5012

Attention organizations, institutions and corporations: This book is available at a quantity discount on bulk purchases for use in education, business, or sales promotion. For information, please contact Kincaid House Publishing at 714.646.6406, or fax to 714.646.7472.

ACKNOWLEDGEMENTS

To thousands of students, clients, teachers and friends who have given support and criticism to the ideas and thoughts expressed in *Full Esteem Ahead*, I thank you.

Special thanks to Glenda, Lorie and Donna for typing and suggesting. Thanks to Silvio, Betty, Dave, Richard and Janice for editorial reviews.

To my mom, thank you for the inspiration that began at such an early age.

And to my wife Lorraine, thank you for your support, your criticism and especially your balance.

To Lisa and Michael, thanks, guys. Thanks for teaching me so much, every day.

The One
in the Glass

When you get what you want in your struggle
     for self
and the world lets you have your own way,
just go to the mirror and look at yourself
and see what that person will say.
For it isn't your father or mother or mate
whose judgment upon you must pass.
The person whose verdict counts most to your
     fate
is the one staring back from the glass.
Some people may think you're a great one
     by gum
and gather to watch you walk by,
but the one in the glass says you're only a bum
if you can't look it straight in the eye.
That's the person to please, never mind the
     rest,
who'll be with you clear up to the end,
and you've passed your most dangerous,
     difficult test
if the one in the glass is your friend.
You may fool the whole world down the
     pathway of years
and get pats on the back as you pass,
but your final reward will be heartaches and
     tears
if you've cheated the one in the glass.

—Author Unknown

CONTENTS

INTRODUCTION

What is self-esteem? Self-esteem is life's bottom line.

Self-esteem is our image of our past, our frame of reference for our present, and our outlook on our future.

Our self-esteem affects our thoughts, our feelings, and our behavior. Asked to define self-esteem, we usually hear phrases like "It's how we feel about ourselves," or "It's my opinion of myself." While not incorrect, neither response offers any sense of the all-encompassing nature of self-esteem.

Self-Esteem is the sum and substance of our feelings and our thoughts about who we are. It is an image we have of ourselves that includes how we got to where we are (developmental), who we are now (in the moment), and who we will be—an assessment of our potential for the future. Self-esteem is a picture of our self which is more comprehensive, more compelling a portrait than could be captured by any photographer or represented by any artist.

This total self-picture is carried in pieces. Some pieces are open to view; some are hidden. At times we view only sections of the picture; at other times we view all we are able to bring to our awareness.

People seek counseling assistance for various problems — addictions, marital problems, loneliness, depression, anger management and other personal issues. These problems are usually of a serious nature, and treatment is often helpful. In most situations the problem presented for treatment is actually a symptom of a greater problem. The real and pervasive problem is low self-esteem. We can no longer afford to treat just symptoms. We must gain a greater understanding of ourselves as individuals and as members of society. In a clinical as well as a societal context, self-esteem must be considered as an individual issue. An understanding and nurturing of our personal values or ethics is essential to our individual growth, and in turn contributes to generally accepted societal standards with a strong moral foundation.

We will here consider various ways of understanding self-esteem. We'll examine where self-esteem comes from. And we'll consider our subconscious mind and how we interact with our self-picture, even when we're not aware we're doing so.

We will then consider self-esteem in a broad, global context. We'll look at keys to strong personal values and a positive self-esteem, and offer some ideas for building and maintaining that positive self-esteem we all seek.

Rob Solomon
Beaverton, Oregon

A Sense
of Your Self

Many psychologists argue that we have developed our self-picture by the time we reach five years of age.

If this were so, we would find ourselves with the same image of ourselves through time, all of our lives. Regardless of how our lives unfold, our self-picture would remain static. When faced with difficulties in our lives, we would be locked into a limited range of responses and be unable to change if it were true that our basic image was unable to be changed.

Faced with problems, we do seek help and we do make changes. Some changes are simply cosmetic; many changes are fundamental, involving deeply held attitudes, protected values, and practiced behaviors.

It is our demonstrated capacity to make significant changes that helps us to see our self-image as a picture which is fluid and constantly subject to change.

By the time we reach age five, our sense of self has developed more substantially than many other facets of our being. A sense of ourselves as a being separate and distinct from our surroundings has come into our awareness.

From the moment we are born, we are dependent. We're dependent upon someone else to feed us, comfort us, and watch over us. We begin to explore our surroundings and, in time, we learn more about our world. We learn about people and things in our world. At about the age of five, we become able to discriminate between ourselves and others. At this point, we've come to understand a key aspect of our existence: that we live as a distinct individual.

"It is our demonstrated capacity to make significant changes that helps us to see our self-image as a picture which is fluid and constantly subject to change."

Our individuality develops as we gain a greater understanding of the nature of our self. We learn what type of individual we are through our relationship with others. Those others give us feedback verbally and by their behavior. The feedback may be direct or indirect, accurate or inaccurate. It is this feedback which serves as a primary tool for building self-knowledge and developing our self-picture.

Parental Influence

In our early years, our greatest contributors to that self-picture and the basis of our self-understanding are our parents. We learn a great deal from our nearly constant interaction with our parents. Our interpretation of that interplay, that verbal and non-verbal communication, can create a fertile, nurturing garden which spawns hardy, vigorous growth, or it can create a barren wasteland where growth is stunted. In most circumstances, parents communicate a wide variety of messages, all of which contribute to the child's self-picture.

Even when interaction with parents is largely positive, there can be messages which a child interprets negatively. When I was in the second grade, our class had spelling tests every week. We would give those tests all our little seven-year-old brains could muster, then we passed our papers to the students behind us to score the tests. Our scored spelling tests were then returned, and we had to take them home to show our parents. A parent had to sign the paper, which we then returned to the teacher.

Not noted, as a youngster, for my spelling skills, it came as a surprise one day when I scored 98 percent on the weekly test. I ran home yelling, "Mom, mom! I got 98 percent on my spelling test!"

She took the paper from my hand, studied it carefully, smiled and said, "What happened to the other 2 percent?"

As another example, a friend, George, was having the guys over to play poker for the evening. That afternoon he took careful inventory and determined a need for potato chips, crackers, cheese and soda pop. George called his eleven-year-old son Colin and asked if he would pick up the groceries, with the admonishment, "And bring back the change!" The boy ran off, returning a short time later and leaving the bag of groceries on the kitchen table. The change was carefully left beside the bag. Dad walked into the kitchen, pocketed his change, and began to empty the bag. "Potato chips, crackers . . . soda . . . soda . . . good God, kid, how stupid can you be? You forgot the cheese!"

These stories are certainly not unusual. They are not stories exclusive to my family or friends. Unfortunately, they are common, and often much more subtle.

What's going on in these stories?

Children are being hurt. As children, we do not hear implied or even intended messages like "I know you could have done better," or "Now someone has to go back to the store." We hear "You didn't do well enough," and "You are stupid." Why are we getting these messages? Is it that so many parents are downright cruel?

Some who study families postulate that parents treat their children the way they were treated as children. We may not have liked the way we were treated as children, but it's the only treatment we saw, so it's the only kind of treatment we ever learned from personal experience. So parents tend to use the same language they heard as kids, threaten the same punishments and promise the same rewards, tell the same stories, and assume the same attitudes.

No one will deny the importance of learned behavior, nor should anyone suggest that parents are anything but powerful teachers. While this is surely part of the answer, parents are not robots unable to think and exercise conscious will over their behavior. Over the last several years, we have been exposed to a variety of warnings concerning how our comments and behavior as parents can impact our children. If we wish to change our responses to our children, we can. We often do. Not all parental communication is hurtful.

Are we back to conscious cruelty? In all but a relatively few cases, no. More often than not we communicate to our children without thinking. George may have had an argument with his wife just before checking the grocery bag's contents. Unresolved anger is easily displaced and finds its way into our communication with others.

Some hurtful messages may be humorous. "What happened to the other 2 percent?" may, if overheard, be judged as a funny quip. But children do not necessarily have so well-developed a sense of humor as their parents do. They see themselves as the object of scorn, and aren't in a position to laugh at the situation.

Displaced anger, misplaced humor—it's all a matter of careless, thoughtless communication. We need to put effort into being aware of what we say, how we say it, and how it's likely to be interpreted. As key painters of our child's self-picture, we need to take care.

These stories are about normal families. Yes, we are talking about the average family, and we're seeing that intrafamily communication isn't always constructive. Often it is neither well thought out, nor received as intended. And that's in caring, loving families. What about abusive families?

Abusive Parents

Statistics suggest that 20 to 30 percent of all children grow up in homes with significant abuse—physical, sexual and/or emotional. Although factors such as the accuracy of reporting and the criteria to define abuse affect such statistics, it appears that many of us were brought up in abusive homes. We can best understand the effect of such an environment on self-esteem development by considering a special and familiar case history.

What comes to mind is the famous case portrayed in *Sybil*, a book and made-for-television movie. The actual real-life Sybil was treated terribly as a child. Her mother would lock her in a closet for days on end without food or water. She was repeatedly beaten and endlessly abused. And how did that on-going trauma affect her? What consequences of such an abhorrent and aberrant upbringing did the adult Sybil manifest? Sybil's reaction to this grossly abusive treatment was to develop not one, but sixteen separate and distinct personalities. Now, dual or multiple personality development in an individual is rare; nevertheless, the dreadful torment through her childhood triggered Sybil to develop sixteen full-blown personalities—complete, separate identities of herself.

When debating why Sybil might have developed so many alternate persons within herself, most observers believe it was her unconscious effort to escape. Most believe she was unconsciously making a frantic effort to escape her cruel and abusive mother; however, Sybil was not escaping her mother, she was seeking to escape herself.

As any child would, Sybil experienced her mother's

behavior toward her as though it was in every way appropriate. How could she have known it was abnormal? There was no one to explain that her mother's treatment of her was far from normal or acceptable. All Sybil understood was that this adult on whom she was totally dependent and of whom she was blindly accepting, was treating her like trash, and that this big person was her mommy, and mommies and daddies are to be obeyed and loved. With that natural, innocent assumption, of course the child Sybil would see her mother's behavior to be correct, rightful and justified.

"The only way any child can view abusive parenting is to believe and accept that they are so 'bad' that they deserve the abuse."

The only way the child—any child—can view abusive parenting is to believe and to accept that they are so "bad" that they deserve the abuse.

Sure, we know that's a totally erroneous conclusion. We know that parents who behave like Sybil's mother are crazy, and that such a child is only a traumatized victim. But we're not children, and we're not dependent on this crazy lady for our basic well being. Nor are we forced to allow such a demented person to dictate our self-picture. Sybil had no choice but to assume that she deserved the treatment she got because she was a terrible person.

We may be comfortable and secure in the knowledge that Sybil's situation and her response to that situation is rare; however, the rarity is only in the extreme nature of her situation. Abuse is shockingly common, and while multiple personality disorders are uncommon, children have severely limited options in their effort to live through the abuse.

Accepting the conclusion that they are responsible for the treatment they received, and therefore are "bad" people, many children's reaction is to withdraw. The withdrawal may take the form of choosing to be alone a lot; it may take the form of having an imaginary playmate, or living in a fantasy world. Or the withdrawal may be extreme, similar to the path Sybil took.

Of course withdrawal is not the only reaction possible. Many children will consciously or unconsciously choose to live up to the label they've accepted. We call their behavior rebellious or "acting out." Ironically, the adult most frustrated by this behavior is most often the abuser, who was actually the instigator of that behavior.

The child's response to abuse and the degree of intensity of that response is related to the intensity of abuse, the nature of the child's self-picture at the time, alternate avenues of support available, and other factors. There is no known formula to predict just how any child will react to abuse. We cannot assume that simply because the abuse is "mild" that the response will be similarly mild, nor can we assume that because the abuse is severe, that the response will be similarly severe.

We can be quite sure that children will tend to internalize abusive behavior, accept the message that they must be deserving of the treatment, and alter their developing self-picture to accommodate the negative input.

If parents were the exclusive influence on our self-esteem development, our efforts to understand the roots of self-esteem would now be complete. The truth is, seeds of our growth come from all directions. From infancy through childhood, we are influenced not only by parents, but by others in the family as well.

Brothers and Sisters

Is it natural for siblings to fight? What parent hasn't asked that question? Natural or not, competition between brothers, between sisters, or between brothers and sisters is certainly common. Often competition is simply an effort to gain the attention of those significant to us. We may be seeking attention from parents, from other family members, or family friends. An only child seeks such attention, too, but does not face the same in-house competition.

The child who finds he must fight a brother or sister cannot help but measure his performance by the feedback he receives about such fighting. We measure our self by feedback from those whose attention we seek, and by the feedback of those we're competing with. If we seem successful in our effort to gain attention, we feel validated or "pretty good" about who we are. The message received is "You are an okay kid/person to be with."

If our efforts fail to attract the attention sought, we'll probably repeat the behavior until the hoped-for reaction is gained, or until something or someone intervenes. If our performance meets with no response—if we get no feedback of any sort—we are devastated. It is widely believed that the pain of being ignored is the worst pain of all.

Perhaps that notion alone explains why children will behave in ways even they know to be inappropriate. They are so much in need of a response from those significant others in their families, in their lives, that they will do whatever they can do to evoke attention.

As mentioned earlier, we also receive messages from those with whom we are in competition. Lisa perceives less attention in her direction than her brother Michael is receiving, and she often picks up the additional message of "Mom likes me best" from her sibling. Michael's message may be direct, or evidenced through play or other indirect communication, but Lisa's reception of the message is real. Mrs. Smothers may or may not have had a preference for one son or the other; however, if such a preference was perceived by either, both Tom and Dick were sure to be affected.

It is fair to assume that most parents make an effort to not favor one child over another. Despite such efforts, every kid in every family is different, and every parent has natural tendencies to favor some traits or some types of behavior over others. Such preferences between children, open or covert, acknowledged or not, are powerful. The effect of preferential attitudes on the part of the parents may well be augmented by the efforts of the competitive sibling as well.

The message may be realistically experienced as "I'm not as good as my brother or sister at shooting baskets, or playing the piano, or running, or drawing," and may be judged to be an acceptable fact of life, which would be extremely healthy. Or the message may well be generalized. We may simply feel inferior, that "I'm not as good/worthy/deserving a person as Sally is."

This attitude may encourage ill feelings between siblings. The child is made to see that these ill feelings are wrongful and inappropriate through direct messages such as "He's your brother, you're supposed to love him" or "She's your sister, you've got to take care of her." The overwhelming response to these messages is likely to be guilt. This feeling that "It's wrong for me to feel this way" only serves to further darken our self-picture. Also, a child feeling this way feels even more inferior to the sibling who was the object of the competition, because it appears to him or her that the sibling isn't troubled with similar feelings towards them.

In these days of multiple marriages, divorces and re-marriages, we often have "blended families."

Children may have step brothers and/or step sisters living full- or part-time in their household. While the competitive dynamic may be similar to the issues between natural siblings, step siblings offer a new, additional challenge.

With the advent of step siblings, the family is redefined, and each child must find and establish his or her place in the new family entity.

The blended family allows an even less stable foundation from which children must define their roles and establish their sense of identity. As the scramble for attention is compounded by the confusion surrounding the family structure, the intensity of the struggle increases.

As children promote their own identity, the temptation is often greater to sacrifice a step sibling, as the children seem to suffer less guilt than they would in so treating a natural sibling.

Bobby thought his sister Diane was okay. They were natural siblings, but when Mom married Rick after divorcing their father, Jason came to live with Bobby and Diane. Jason was perceived as an intruder. Mom could choose to marry Rick if that's what she wanted, but why should Bobby and Diane have to alter their living circumstances and put up with Jason? Besides, Jason was a constant reminder that their real Dad wasn't coming back, and would never be part of the family again. Jason became an easy scapegoat every time Diane or Bobby needed one. It was a comfortable place to put anger, and, though Jason tried to fight back, he was outnumbered and overwhelmed. He lost many battles, which adversely affected his self-esteem. He often felt hurt and alone.

It's tremendously important for parents and step-parents to make sure in every possible way that each child, biological or step, feels as loved and valued as the other children in the family.

Grandparents, aunts, uncles—any family member spending a considerable time with us—will have influences on our self-image, and will add detail to our emerging self-picture. As we grow, we tend to increase our circle of people with whom we interact. We become more involved with our peers.

Friends

As a television host in the 1950s, Art Linkletter was peerless as an interviewer of children. He wrote a book about his experiences with kids on the air, entitled *Kids Say the Darndest Things*. Well, that they do. But sometimes what kids say to other kids isn't funny at all, but is often distinctly cruel, and calculated to hurt. One common area in which kids are verbally mean to other kids is the nicknames they choose to saddle them with.

Many of us have grown up with nicknames we would never have chosen for ourselves. Why are kids stuck with names such as *Fatty* or *Fats, Schnozz, Dogface* and *Meathead?* There's the story of the famous mobster of the forties and fifties, Ben (Bugsy) Siegel. It is reputed that the egocentric, charming and murderous gangster hated the nickname *Bugsy*, which was given him by his playmates when he was a kid because he collected bugs, but couldn't shake it.

Have you ever noticed how quick kids are (even quicker than many adults we might assess as bigots) to label other children with racial epithets like *nigger* or *wop* or *kike?* Is it hatefulness and cruelty ?

Many feel that this is learned behavior. Kids who label others negatively learned it from their parents. The parent may be victimizing others out of displaced anger, but the child, through repeated exposure, learns not only that it is apparently appropriate behavior, but also that he or she may find some relief from their own unexpressed anger. Perhaps this is a sound explanation.

Some suggest that kids put others down because it makes them feel better about themselves. By casting a disparaging label on someone else, one implies that he or she is superior. Undoubtedly this explains

"We see our membership in and acceptance by various groups as self-validating and self-enhancing."

some of the negative labeling among peers.

These put-downs are seldom found in one-on-one inter-actions. Most appear to take place in a group context, and are often based on a person's need to belong. All of us, children and adults, have a strong need to belong. We need to see ourselves as associated with various groups in order to understand much of our own identity. The groups act as a kind of mirror, reflecting our own image back to ourself. We see our membership in and acceptance by various groups as self-validating and self-enhancing.

Early in our development we fight hard to individuate—to discover ourselves as separate beings. As we grow older and more complex, in the pre-teen and adolescent years, we seek to further define ourselves in a group context.

Much analysis is being done on the problem of youth gangs and their increasing prevalence in America. There is widespread agreement that a gang serves as a surrogate family, where a member can feel surrounded by and sup-ported by "brothers," even when his birth family is dys-functional or simply no longer answering his needs.

One very successful way to engineer our membership into a group is to identify a common enemy, using that person or persons as a target. If we can get three of our peers to agree that Johnny is a little twerp and a crybaby whom we all should avoid, then we have just joined the "We won't hang around Johnny" group.

"The consequences for those who are spurned are certainly destructive and may well prove to be disasterous."

Traditional enemies can be-come fast friends when faced with a common threat. The motiva-tion is usually self-serving. The joining may well be self-enhanc-ing and a positive component for one's self-picture development. It's seen as proof of belonging. The consequences for those who are spurned and not allowed into the group are certainly destructive, and may well prove to be disasterous.

The opportunity to join with peers, to learn how to bond with others, and to be accepted, is an integral building block for a positive self-picture. Most of us have been welcomed by some groups and cast off by others. We form a great deal of self-understanding and perhaps misunderstanding through our peer interactions as children, and as adults.

As we grow our interaction increases, and we widen our circle of associates or friends. We spend less time with our immediate family and more time with others. We become involved with the education system.

Schools

Teachers, the foundation of the education system, are generally dedicated folk wishing to asssist with children's intellectual development. Most are concerned with the whole child, and in addition to teaching today's version of the old *Three Rs*, will make an effort to help the child to develop strong values and a positive sense of self.

It is true, though, that teachers are often pressed with the demands of the educational system. There are overloaded classrooms, tons of paperwork, extracurricular responsibilities, budget limitations, and more. Realistically, it is difficult for teachers to offer much more than the necessary instruction to most students in their charge. There may be some time for those showing the most need, but the majority are often "hustled through the system." The resulting lack of individual attention is in itself dehumanizing. Our self-picture, while not assaulted by the system, is unfortunately seldom enhanced by it. Those who gain attention, rewards and esteem-enhancing moments are those students who stand out due either to outstanding performance, or an obvious need for assistance. The message for the majority is, at best, benign. For some students, the message is a hard-hitting one: "You are just one of many. There is nothing special about you."

Educators who are able to connect with students and assist them in their efforts to develop their individual skills are successful in combating the dehumanizing aspects of the system. While there are many such teachers who are so dedicated and so able, the need to increase their ranks is gargantuan. Educators in general do the best they can.

In the system, it is not surprising that many teachers respond to students' demands in a curt and unthinking manner. Teachers are human, too, and are often stressed by the system, and frustrated by the students' performance, or the lack thereof. How many teachers, knowing that the student is achieving less than he has been deemed capable of, respond with "You're just not living up to your potential"? These teachers are attempting to be encouraging. They are trying to tell us to perform as well as we can. Yet students tend to hear "You're just not doing well enough." Perhaps they are not studying as diligently as they might. Perhaps they're not paying attention as closely as they could. Although it is possible to expect a student to say "You're right, and I will try harder," most students are likely to respond silently, and negatively.

When we hear that we're not doing as well as we should, our defenses tend to take over. Realistic or not, we often respond with "I'm doing as well as I can. If the teacher can't see that, well, I just won't bother to try anymore."

Most people aren't always aware of their shortcomings. We're most likely to believe our self-talk which says we are doing the very best we can. Faced with this belief and the authoritative input to the contrary, we have two alternative responses.

We might accept that there are some things we could do differently, seek help in our efforts to improve and, rising to the challenge laid before us, improve our performance.

We are more likely to choose to give up. It is very easy to conclude that if our best isn't good enough, there is no point in trying our best. We receive no recognition for our efforts, we earn only admonishment, and we respond with an attitude of defeat. Such defeat carries a message more generic than performance in the educational system. The message is one of general hopelessness, which increases our sense of frustration, and which in turn tends to infect many or most of our endeavors and activities.

"Such defeat carries a message more generic than performance in the educational system."

This negative and self-defeating message is most often internalized as "I am not being the person I am capable of being. I'm missing the mark. There must be something wrong with me." The message becomes another component in our self-image.

The wide range of experiences a student has while going through school—scholastic, athletic, social, emotional—all constitute input to his or her self-esteem development. Each of these elements adds to the emerging self-pictures of each student. The achievements and successes gained, or the failures and the contests lost, and the varied feedback those experiences generate, including how they're handled by authority figures, make their imprint.

As we explore these elements of influence—parents, siblings and other family members, peers, educators and more—we must bear in mind that we have options in how we process and store the feedback we receive. While we are active participants in the development of our self-esteem, our environment offers its influences with varying degrees of forcefulness.

The Joneses

Just as we are influenced by our peers as children, we are influenced by our friends and neighbors as we grow older. The concept of "keeping up with the Joneses" is a very real phenomenon. Many of us measure our standing in the world by comparison with others. Am I making as much money as Nancy is? Do I dress as well as the guys at the club? Is my haircut the latest trend?

We ask these questions, or questions like them, constantly. Many seek answers by looking at people they know and comparing what they see of those people's progress, or success, to their own. The main problem is, our perceptions of others may be accurate, or they may be inaccurate. And of course we can't possibly have sufficient information to verify our perceptions of what appears on the surface. The old Native American expression about not judging others until you've walked in their moccasins goes both ways. Sure your friend's husband looks much more appealing when you don't have to pick up his socks. Of course the woman ensconced in the proverbial mansion on the hill seems enviable when you can't view her loneliness.

But even when based on inaccurate perceptions, these messages contribute to our self-esteem. We evaluate the information, and rate ourselves as to doing better or worse. If we rate ourselves better, we accept a positive element for our developing image. If in our estimation we don't make the grade, we add negative components to that picture.

While this kind of comparison obviously has flaws, we do it. We learn much of our comparison skills from the competitive nature of the educational system, and those lessons are reinforced by the media. As potent an element as our friends and co-workers may be, perhaps the most constant and oppressive influence is found all around us, every day, in the media. Television, radio, newspapers, magazines and motion pictures unendingly bombard us with information which calls forth a multitude of messages which we process and file away, and which we will later retrieve, consciously or unconsciously.

The Mass Media

Some time ago a national hair care company developed an ingenious advertising campaign to market hair coloring products. While all marketing efforts are directed at convincing people to purchase products or services, this particular campaign and its catchy slogan, "Is it true blondes have more fun?" is especially clever in planting the suggestion that, if a woman were to use the hair coloring product and become a blonde, she'd have more fun. Have you ever met anyone who would say they are having all the fun they can possibly handle? So how could any woman deny herself the prospect of more fun in her life? The beauty of this classic advertising campaign is that it appeals not only to those with low self-esteem, but to women at all levels of the self-esteem scale.

Whether our esteem is so low that we can't remember ever having had any fun, or we feel pretty darned good about ourselves, it's difficult to imagine a negative response to the enticing question posed by the advertiser in this example.

You'll hear many people sneer, "Who believes that stuff?" It's true that the advertising messages are often not consciously believed by consumers; we know that there is no guarantee if we purchase this gadget or that car that we will find a significant improvement in our

"But what about our subconscious? Are we strong enough emotionally to deny the hope inherent in that message?"

lives. Of course we know this intellectually. But what about our subconscious? Are we strong enough emotionally to deny the *hope* inherent in that message?

Can we resist the mass media messages that suggest we will be strong and virile men if we smoke some cattle-rustling brand of cigarette—or that we'll be progressive, liberated, assertive women if we smoke some slim brand? Don't we unconsciously get drawn into the belief that drinking a particular beer will lead to greater romantic success in our lives? If we wish to see ourselves as independent, liberated, attractive women, must we drive a particular model of car?

We are educated consumers, are we not? We're not a bunch of fools. Society today is certainly more advanced and generally more sophisticated than ever before. As consumers with a high level of awareness, surely we can dismiss the mass media's idealized role models as simply hype to sell heaps of products. Right?

The truth is, we cannot resist these messages. We can't resist the messages, because the advertising industry has found our Achilles heel: we're human, with all the common frailties. Most of us are pretty well educated, and some of us may be very polished and quite worldly; nonetheless, we are all beset with needs. The need to feel better about ourselves is universal. And we can't take away from those advertising creative types; superceding their own human frailties and lists of needs are the tricks of the trade that have become a science, and that they've learned very well. They know how to sell. It's what keeps business in business.

We can't look at advertisers as evil ogres who prey on those of us with low self-esteem. Actually they address the great cross section of humanity, gearing to whatever slice or segment of the population they deem as their target demographic group for any given product. But the "hot button" most commonly used to sell goods and services—and jeans and cruises and cosmetics and yogurt—is our innate desire for self improvement. Just as every person is interested in having more fun, we are all interested in feeling better, looking better, living better, and being more successful.

Advertising is not the only area of modern life contributing to the constant bombardment of self-esteem messages. Isn't the subject matter of movies, television, and the print media often those "human interest" characters who possess something we would like to possess? The "up close and personal" profiles of the hot celebrities and eccentric dilettantes—does the term *Lifestyles of the Rich and Famous* ring a bell?—always generate strong audience response. Such profiles highlight achievements or attributes, and sometimes shortcomings and tragic flaws. But what many people do when they view or read such stories is, compare themselves to these celebrities. Of course they'll never come close to meeting such superhuman standards; therefore, they internalize more negative input.

Some experts suggest that magazines and tabloids that focus on "the dirt," fact or fiction, about celebrities are popular due to our voyeuristic tendencies. What are we "voyeurs" looking for? We're looking to establish models for our own personal expectations and goals. We may be seeking to feel better about our own situation by learning that others are worse off than we are. Our voyeurism is rooted in our desire to relate the situations of others to our self, to our own lot in life.

To round out this overview of the source for news, information and entertainment which we call the media, we should also consider books. Non-fiction, like the book you're reading right now, is obviously for gathering specific information. But fiction affords entertainment and diversion. This diversion is also often self-esteem related. We read about characters who are flawed and note with satisfaction that we would have handled the adventure better. Or we read about characters who appear flawless and wish we were as they appear to be.

It's important to note that we are not controlled by the media. The media, at least in most countries, do not overtly tell us how to act, what to think, who we should be, or what we should be doing. But the media do interact with other factors on which we base or build our self-esteem. The media assist us in our efforts to measure our needs, wants, and our progress. Our interpretaton of media input may be detrimental or beneficial, just as our interpretation of other esteem factors may prove positive or negative. At any given moment, the messages we pick up from the media may serve to enhance our self-image, attack it, or preserve its status quo.

". . .the messages we pick up from the media may serve to enhance our self-image, attack it, or preserve its status quo."

While we are generally aware as to the potential of the media to influence us, few are aware of the number of messages constantly received by our subconscious. We may believe that media images have little bearing on our self-assessment. We know we are resistant to specific messages about using a particular product, even though the image presented is a desired image for us. While that is true, the resistance is conscious. Even though we may not succumb to the pitch and buy the product, the message can have a residual effect. We are left with a reminder. We may not buy the product in an effort to gain that desired image, but we remain reminded that that we do not have all we want. This is a significant negative message to our ever-developing self picture: "If only I was good/worthy/deserving, I'd have what I want."

We must be concerned not only with messages received consciously, but subconsciously as well. While we recognize the issue of subliminal messages in advertising and acknowledge the inherent dangers and insidious suggestions, the issue of messages purposely hidden from our awareness by advertisers with questionable scruples is not a major concern, because there are now laws to protect us from such deceit and trickery. There is however a need to recognize that there are messages which, though not expressly hidden from us by others, are received without our awareness at the time.

Every day, in every area of every person's life, information which influences us is taken in subconsciously—from the media, the "Joneses," friends and family. In a later chapter, we'll explore the subconscious mind and the consequences of this information more fully.

As we've been demonstrating, there is a multitude of factors helping us to develop our self-picture. Organized religion, any religion, is a potent element.

Religion

Religions offer a prescription for living. Religion can offer us a way in which to structure our lives, and provide a framework for understanding the life that unfolds. Organized religion can provide comfort and can offer a foundation for growth. As a guide, religion gives us a way in which we can measure our selves and understand our developmental progress.

Organized religion may also serve up messages which cause devastation and despair to susceptible individuals.

Let us consider that which forms a credo for many organized religions: the Ten Commandments. Intended as a directive for how life should be lived, the Commandments are themselves a set of criteria against which we can measure our growth and development. Fine. But that means they are a standard of excellence to strive for, not a dictate or an imperative, the breaking of which would be grounds for punishment or eternal damnation. As the old, anonymous saying goes, *Errare humanum est.* To err is human. Who hasn't broken any of the Ten Commandments? Most of us have broken at least one of the Commandments at some time or other in our lives.

If the organized religion to which we subscribe has given us the unqualified message that these Commandments must never, under any circumstances, be broken, we may very well be left with the message that we are damned without hope of redemption. We may choose to interpret such religious prescriptions as the way we must live *or else*, and by doing so, face the penalty of being worthless for all time. Such a message does not encourage positive self-esteem.

Surely religion in and of itself is not destructive. Faith and belief in God or some power greater than humanity is a comfort, and may serve our efforts to move toward a positive self-image. As for so many of these esteem factors, it is not the factor itself, it is how we interpret the esteem-related messages garnered consciously and unconsciously.

All the factors, all the roots of self-esteem discussed to this point, are largely external. Although the true impact of these factors is measured by the impact they have when internalized, the factors or elements originate outside of us.

A crucial element of self-esteem, based on our own perceptions and judgments, lies within each of us. The essence of how we see our behavior is called our Personal Performance Ratio.

Personal Performance Ratio

The Personal Performance Ratio is the mechanism each of us uses to rate our performance in a given situation. The Performance Ratio is the process of applying our expectations and values to our behavior in an effort to evaluate that behavior. Was it good? Was it bad? Was I successful? Was I appropriate?

To establish expectations, we apply the sum total of our previous experiences that we perceive as being related to the task at hand. We predict our level of performance prior to our effort, and we establish judgmental criteria through the application of our expectations.

The degree of importance we place on a given task is a crucial element in the Performance Ratio. Our expectations of performance dictate a grading system, which yields a "score" for our performance, just as an accepted set of standards dictates the grading system by which Olympic divers and gymnasts and ice skaters are judged. The value we place on the behavior determines the impact the score will have on our self-esteem, much as the degree of difficulty of the dive, the exercise or the routine impacts the score given to the athlete.

"We predict our level of performance prior to our effort, and we establish judgmental criteria through the application of our expectations."

Roger is 17 years old, living at home with his parents. One of Roger's most dreaded household chores is vacuuming. He hates it. And he's expected to vacuum the house every week.

When Roger completes this personal pain-in-the-neck, Roger's mother offers her appraisal. "Not too bad this time, Roger. I'd give it about a six out of ten. You could do better." Now, Roger would have given his effort a seven on the same point scale. He may hate the task, but he still has a set of criteria with which to judge the job he did. A seven is Roger's Performance Ratio. It doesn't matter that the external feedback—his mother's score of six—was less; it matters only that Roger believes his appraisal to be accurate.

Roger's score for his vacuuming performance provides direct internal feedback. It may be somewhat affected by external input like his Mom's score or his Dad's comments about missing the corners, but the score that counts the most is the direct one—of, by and for Roger.

In this case, Roger's Performance Ratio is not very meaningful to him, nor to his self-esteem, because he places no value on the task.

On the other hand, Roger is an avid dirt bike rider. He lives for hitting the hills, exploring new terrain, and especially for jumping—over streams, rivers, gorges, whatever he happens upon. He's been riding for three years, and he's confident he can clear almost any 15-foot jump with minimal effort.

One day, out in the local foothills, Roger discovers a new stream. He assesses the distance across to be about 12 feet. He steadies himself, guns the throttle, makes the jump and lands safely across the stream. He scores himself a six. Yes, he made it, but he fully expected to. It was easy.

Another day in the hills and another jump—this time over a dry creekbed—he misses the opposite bank and lands in the rocks. He didn't make the jump, though it was the same 12-foot distance he made the last outing. He scores a minus one. He expected to make the jump easily, but he missed.

Weeks later Roger is out on a different trail and comes across a river. He judges the distance across to be about 20 feet. He's only sure of jumping around 15 feet, but decides to go for it. He makes it! He's thrilled! He gives himself a perfect ten. He didn't expect to make the jump, but he did. But what if he had missed the 20-foot jump? He still might score himself a six or a seven, because he honestly didn't expect to make the jump, but gave himself credit for trying, for facing a new challenge. Only a perfectly successful jump could score him a ten, but trying is worth a lot.

It's to Roger's tremendous advantage to realize the value of trying. Dirt bike jumping is important to him, and he's seeing rapid improvement. An honestly-earned high score on one's Personal Performance Ratio on a task which is highly valued has a powerful positive impact on Roger's self-esteem. Conversely, a low Performance Ratio based on a similarly enjoyed and valued behavior would have a negative influence on his self-esteem. But even a perfect ten on vacuuming would have little impact on Roger's self-esteem.

When we attempt a task, we do so with expectations of success or failure. Based on those expectations, along with our actual performance results, we score our effort. We credit success, but we surely give points for trying, for stretching.

If we avoid attempting for fear of failure, we still yield a score, but it is a negative one. Avoiding a challenge gives us the message that we just can't handle whatever task is at issue, that we're "chicken" or wimpy. Unless the task is truly impossible or highly improbable, choosing to avoid an attempt yields negative input to our self-image. It is vital to try. Making an attempt counts greatly.

"Based on those expectations, along with our actual performance results, we score our effort. We credit success, but we surely give points for trying, for stretching."

The degree of importance we place upon the behavior establishes the power the message will carry. If it's important, it will enhance our self-esteem when we do well and can give ourselves a high score. But if we don't care for or about the task, even a positive Performance Ratio has little or no impact.

In relation to all our behavior, when we combine our Performance Ratio, in measurement of our results, with the personal importance factor, the resulting "score" is a message that becomes a component of our self-image. Positive or negative, its impact is very powerful.

Your Hidden Self

Let us consider the human being. Let us consider the magical components—skin and bone and blood and muscles and organs and nerves and minds—which make up people like you and me and Attila the Hun and Mother Teresa. We have what could be called a "physical plant"—all those things which work together to make the wonderous human body work. And we have the intangibles of intellect, character, and emotions.

One of the most important ways to consider individual human beings is to recognize that each human being has two essential component parts to his or her non-physical, or mental, being. Each of us has a conscious mind and a subconscious mind. While different psychological theorists assign different labels and perhaps even different levels to consciousness, it is generally accepted that there is at least the conscious component and the subconscious component to the human mind.

We can consider the conscious mind to be the reservoir of information, attitudes, feelings, and all mental faculties which we are aware of possessing. The subconscious mind

38

—your hidden self—represents that area in which we store information, attitudes, feelings and emotions that for one reason or another we place out of our awareness.

Often, information simply travels to our subconscious and stays there (or goes wherever unneeded information goes) because we recognize no need to retain it. Sometimes we receive information which we endeavor to place into our subconscious, so that we need not deal with it. Sometimes, information is received by our subconscious, and will travel back and forth to our conscious, depending upon the nature of the information and our personal desire to process and act upon the information, or not to process and handle it.

Useless Information

Perhaps the most common reason for information received by our conscious mind to be buried or deposited into our subconscious mind is that the information is deemed to be useless, or at least unimportant, to us.

If you are one of many North Americans who regularly watches half-hour- to hour-long news programs with innumerable "sound bites" of thirty to sixty seconds in length, you are exposed to a great deal of information which many people claim is news. You deem certain things to be important and relevant, and of enough concern to store in your conscious mind. You wish to be aware about certain things. Many other stories and pieces of information from those telecasts are deemed irrelevant to your current needs and wants, and therefore must be deposited elsewhere. If you were to maintain awareness of all the information on those newscasts, plus all the information you receive through your senses every day, every hour, you would go crazy. Sociologists refer to the overabundance of information in today's modern society as "information overload."

Victims of information overload lose perspective and may become confused as to the nature of reality. We must filter out extraneous information in order to avoid overload, and to function effectively in our complex world. As the information comes to us, we may not simply discard it; however, if we remove it from our awareness, we have succeeded in developing our protection from such an overload. Should we deem information useless, and as a result deposit it into our subconscious, is it possible in different circumstances to retrieve that information and bring it to our conscious mind?

"Victims of information overload lose perspective and may become confused as to the nature of reality."

Should a piece of information which we choose to store in our subconscious (due to its apparent irrelevancy) become relevant, often we cannot find it in our subconscious. Sometimes we are tormented in our attempts to retrieve information; we bemoan the fact with phrases like "It's on the tip of my tongue," which reflects that indeed we have stored the information somewhere, but cannot pull it up at will. Given time, patience, and effort, we may retrieve the information on our own. At times we may seek assistance to jolt our subconscious and bring that information back to our conscious minds—much like an old song or a particular scent will jar a perfectly vivid memory of something that happened years ago.

Threat and Defenses

At times it is our judgment that information is not useful and we therefore decide to discard it or place it into our subconscious. And sometimes we decide that certain information is in some way too upsetting for us to recognize and accept at the time the information is received, so it, too, is tucked into the subconscious.

Information that threatens us, or in some way calls for us to change the way we see things or the way we behave, is most likely information we would work to avoid. The degree to which we are invested in perceiving things the way we already do and/or behaving the way that we are, dictates the degree of threat that we percieve in the new information. Should we perceive a high degree of threat, we will utilize processes known as *defense mechanisms* to protect ourselves from that perceived threat.

These defense mechanisms, perhaps originally coined by Sigmund Freud as *ego defense mechanisms*, take the form of projection, rationalization, denial, and many other processes. The common characteristic of defense mechanisms is that they enable us to maintain our desired ignorance concerning events or occurrences considered upsetting. They cause us to ignore the information, or delay our conscious reception of it.

> *"These defense mechanisms ... take the form of projection, rationalization, denial, and many other processes."*

For one reason or another, we have determined that the information presented is not appropriate for us at this time. We may choose to defer the information and place it into our subconscious, or that choice may be made outside of our own awareness. The decision to place information into our subconscious is most often done at a subconscious level. The motivation for storing the information in our subconscious is quite understandable with the paraphrasing of the old adage, "Out of sight, out of mind," to read "Out of conscious mind, no longer a threat."

Are defense mechanisms healthy, or unhealthy? Yes.

Is the process of storing upsetting information a positive or negative process? Yes.

Consider the case of Harold and Lilly. Harold and Lilly

are 80 and 79 years old respectively, and have been married for 55 years. They have shared so much together they are like human ditto marks.

One morning Lilly wakes up, reaches over to Harold, and Harold does not respond. Lilly shakes him a little bit more forcefully and still no response. Lilly gets up out of bed, reaches for the phone and calls the family doctor. Explaining the situation to the doctor, she is advised to call an ambulance. The ambulance comes and confirms the fact: Harold is dead.

A few days later, Lilly attends the funeral services for Harold, surrounded by family and friends. Following the burial, she goes home and makes lunch for two. She eats one lunch and lets the other sit. The phone rings and the caller asks to speak to Harold. Lilly replies that Harold isn't in at the moment, but she'd be happy to take a message, and a message is taken.

Lilly makes dinner, again for two. Later, Lilly goes to sleep. She wakes up, says good morning to Harold, and makes breakfast, for two. Later, while doing housework, the radio is on. Over the station she hears "their song." Immediately upon hearing this familiar music Lilly bursts into tears. She cries, "My dear Harold's dead. What am I going to do?"

Lilly was consciously aware of Harold's death the morning she awoke and called the doctor. She reacted to the situation in a normal, well-thought-out manner. She arranged for the burial and attended the funeral. Yet she felt unable to deal with the information, the loss of her beloved spouse, and stored the information in her subconscious. It was the strains of the familiar music on the radio that prompted her to *consciously* accept the information that was bubbling underneath that line of awareness which separates the conscious mind from the subconscious. The dreaded, heartbreaking information was stored away until she was ready to accept it. The combination of time for her conscious mind to prepare for the acceptance of the reality, and the gentle persuasion of the favorite song, allowed Lilly to accept the loss in a way that was most appropriate for her, and in her own time. She took time to get centered, so she could cope.

One could argue that the use of the defense mechanism known as denial, in this case, helped Lilly to emotionally prepare for the acceptance of the loss of her husband and thereby encouraged the beginning of the necessary grieving process. If Lilly had been unable to utilize a defense mechanism to delay that acceptance, it is likely that she would have found herself lost in emotion, fraught with fears and self-destructive attitudes, and perhaps faced with self-destructive behavior. Had she not been able to delay the acceptance of her husband's death until she felt centered and safe, the results may well have been devastating. In this case, it appears obvious that the defense mechanism was clearly very, very healthy. Yes, it resulted in the unnecessary preparation of meals, and the providing of false information to the caller inquiring after Harold; nevertheless, all of these consequences were ultimately insignificant compared to Lilly's need to remain stable and healthy.

Breaking Denial

However, if the defense mechanism had stored the information in the subconscious for a protracted period of time, enabling Lilly to develop a long-term fantasy that her husband was alive and involved in her life, it is generally accepted that such a fantasy would have been quite destructive. Counseling assistance of one kind or another would be appropriate in such a situation in order to *break through the denial* and assist Lilly in her effort to accept the reality.

Breaking denial is often discussed in chemical dependency situations. Often a chemically dependent individual (see Chapter 4) will have and generate problems due to his or her chemical use. In the example of the stereotypical male alcoholic, he is generally abusive, if not physically, certainly emotionally, to his wife and family, irresponsible, and in many ways destructive. A commonly accepted symptom of the disease of alcoholism is labeled *denial*. This is a condition in which all those around the alcoholic can see the problems generated by drinking and recognize the destructive nature of his drinking, but he can't. The alcoholic himself is in denial. The alcoholic is aware that he is drinking, but cannot see any problems connected to that drinking.

The alcoholic cannot see the problems caused by his drinking? Of course not. The alcoholic does not wish to see those problems. As a result, the alcoholic buries the knowledge of those problems in his subconscious. The alcoholic sees any acknowledgment or acceptance of the problems connected to his drinking as being a terrible threat to his status quo. As much as the drinking is causing problems, the alcoholic drinks because he gains some reward for his drinking, be it a physiologically based reward or a psychologically based reward. Even if his reward is avoiding the pain and discomfort of withdrawal, rewards work against incentive to change behavior. We fear the consequences of change. In this vein, any acknowledgement of alchoholism and the resultant necessity to quit drinking is totally unacceptable. It is a threat.

"The process of enabling an alcoholic to accept his alcoholism is referred to as breaking the denial."

The process of enabling an alcoholic to accept his alcoholism is referred to as *breaking the denial.*

It is generally agreed that an alcoholic who fails to accept his or her alcoholism is doomed to continue on a path of self-destruction and the destruction of those around him or her until such time as the denial can be broken. The defense mechanisms that operate to help the alcoholic maintain his alcoholic behavior are counterproductive, destructive mechanisms.

The current situation in North American society of rampant drug use and abuse among children is another opportunity to consider the relevance of defense mechanisms and the way they operate.

In schools the issue of drug abuse is of concern to staff, parents, and students. Defense mechanisms are evident among parents when contacted to participate in drug prevention programs. Although most parents will acknowledge that drug use is rampant among junior and senior high school students, the phenomenon of "not *my* kid" appears to be equally as rampant as the drug epidemic itself.

The phrase "we'll deny it even if there are pictures" seems to be relevant here. Parents may learn about drug abuse in general—note the presence of various drug-related paraphernalia in their child's bedroom, and observe that the child chooses to associate with children who are perceived to be drug users. Yet in the face of specific information in support of these facts, parents will continue with "not *my* kid." When the child states, "the stuff belongs to a friend," many of the parents will choose to believe the lie.

While it is obvious that not every child is a drug abuser, the concept of one's own child being a drug user implies, to so many parents, such a great degree of personal failure in parenting that they will refuse to accept the notion that their child may in fact be involved with drugs. If their child is experimenting with drugs or using heavily, this attitude is obviously counterproductive. The attitude is maintained through defense mechanisms, enabling the parents to bury the information concerning the presence of drug paraphernalia and the type of kids with whom their children choose to associate. All such information is buried in subconscious of the parents, because they cannot and will not accept the possibility that their child is drug-involved.

The fact that this drug involvement is very seldom the direct fault or responsibility of the parents is not relevant. The fact that the parents will perceive such drug involvement as a personal failure is by far the most relevant issue leading to the placement of such painful and discriminating information into the subconscious. If the problem exists and is denied by members of the family, this is obviously counterproductive. Unless the problem is acknowledged and accepted, no help can be made available to any of the people involved.

"Unless the problem is acknowledged and accepted, no help can be made available to any of the people involved."

Defense mechanisms can therefore be productive or counterproductive, depending upon the situation. One can argue that defense mechanisms are nature's way of enabling human beings to cope with unpleasant realities. As with any skill, when used excessively and indiscriminately, defense mechanisms may prove harmful and counterproductive. It is difficult for anyone to monitor his or her own applications of defense mechanisms when so much in this regard is done subconsciously.

Emotional information that is unpleasant to us is often stored in the subconscious. If we receive information from our parents, teachers, the media, or anywhere else that suggests we are inferior or not worthwhile as people, we can choose to consciously accept this information and deal with it. But the natural tendency appears to be to deny the information in order to deny having to work through it and all that it indicates. If one accepts the information because it comes from sources which one respects, it calls for a great deal of energy to deal effectively with the information. One needs to consider the rationale for the respect of the source, to evaluate the information, and to respond to the threat of change implied or required by the information. One may need to choose alternate manners of behavior, and go through all the effort that decision would entail. Of course, the path of least resistance is most often chosen. People tend to put information that is uncomplimentary into their subconscious.

It is not only facts that we often choose to avoid. We can sometimes effectively deny feelings. And sometimes the facts of a matter are accepted, but feelings relating to those facts are buried away.

A surface consideration of the phenomenon would suggest that if people are putting facts and/or feelings out of their awareness, there is indeed no problem. After all, haven't we always heard that "what we don't know can't hurt us"? This could perhaps be a viable, effective use of the defense mechanism phenomenon. As with sweet little Lilly above, the defense mechanism can delay the unpleasant reality until we are able to adequately deal with it. On the other hand, if Lilly had continued to deny the realtity of her beloved husband's death for an ongoing period of time, she would have sunk into a foggy world of unreality, and would therefore have been in an unhealthy mental state.

As a wise man once said, for every problem there is a solution that is obvious, simple, straight-forward, and wrong. The act of placing information that is upsetting to our self-concept, and indeed threatens our self-concept, into our subconscious indefinitely is an example of such a solution.

Subconscious Behaviors

When people place upsetting information into their subconscious, although by definition it lies out of their awareness, it does not mean that information will have no effect on their attitudes, feelings, and behavior.

The information is indeed buried out of awareness. The emotions attached to that information are also buried. If the information is upsetting, the upset feeling and associated anger and/or sadness is buried along with the information. At times, just as we retain the information consciously, we send the emotion we've decided to avoid to rest in our subconscious. Although out of our awareness, the emotion is real and will haunt us from time to time, via our attitudes, our behavior, or in some other way.

How many times have we found ourselves worried but unsure as to exactly what is troubling us? How many times have we found ourselves angry but not really sure just what it is we're angry about? Often we will express anger with a particular individual, yet all the while knowing that the anger we're expressing is largely unwarranted, or by all indications simply out of proportion.

Take for instance the situation of a child misbehaving. Your five-year-old spills his milk. This is a situation in which most parents would get somewhat angry and/or disappointed. They might say, "Come on, Michael, you know better than that. You'd better clean up the milk, and be careful not to do it again." Occasionally a parent may yell, "Michael! How could you be so damn stupid? You know better than that. What kind of an idiot are you?!" Upon reflection, that parent, following that incident, is well aware that his anger was out of proportion. It may be a direct result of the time when that parent was five years old, spilled milk, and was disciplined out of proportion to the accident. The anger and frustration over having been so disciplined rests in that parent's subconscious, triggered by reliving the incident. Because the recollection of the incident, as well as the emotions attached to it, are resting in the subconscious, the parent's response is governed by emotions inappropriate to the situation, and not understood by the parent, much less the child. Had the parent recalled the incident but denied the associated feelings, the same excessive anger response would have been the likely result.

Let's consider Tom. Typically when Tom fights with his

wife Leslie, he doesn't feel he can resolve the anger with her, so he chooses to cool off by taking a walk. On a night when such a fight prompts his cooling-off walk, Tom chooses to walk into a bar and order a drink. The person on the stool next to him accidentally knocks Tom's arm, causing Tom to spill his drink. Tom responds by punching this person, a man he doesn't even know, in the nose. Tom doesn't acknowledge that the issue is displaced anger, specifically anger which he's buried in his subconscious, and which would be better directed toward his spouse and resolved. It is clear that Tom's anger-based response to the man in the bar was certainly more than was justified by the stranger's accidental behavior.

Feelings buried in our subconscious affect our behavior.

In addition to behavioral considerations, attitudinal considerations are also important. My client John constantly buries in his subconscious information that suggests personal negative self-worth. He works hard to ignore issues that hurt his self-concept in order to avoid uncomfortable inner conflict. By doing so, John allows himself to perform on a daily basis those tasks that are necessary and essential to living. His social skills are not endangered. However, the capacity for enjoying life, and indeed the capacity for growth, is severely restricted.

"Feelings buried in our subconscious affect our behavior."

While it comes as no surprise that folks with a negative self-image have a restricted capacity for growth and enjoyment of life, the tragedy in this case is that when the information suggesting negative self-worth is buried out of the individual's awareness, it has its effect, but the individual cannot understand why.

When the individual looks at his life and sees his daily situation as being not bad, or even better than not bad, yet still has this rather vague awareness of not feeling very good about himself—having low self-esteem—the person wonders why. Why do I feel this way? Why am I unhappy? The answer may be a complex systemic issue. It may be that while the individual was growing up, his or her parents suggested—through words, actions, or inaction—that he or she was not a worthy person. That being the case, though the individual effectively buried that information into the subconscious, he or she would still be affected by it. The effect of this information is not the main concern; the lack of awareness as to where these feelings and attitudes are coming from is the troublesome issue.

"The awareness of the nature of feelings of low self-esteem resting in the individual's subconscious is a major step toward personal growth."

The awareness of the nature of feelings of low self-esteem resting in the individual's subconscious is a major step toward personal growth.

A Call for Awareness

In our efforts to establish and maintain a positive sense of self-esteem, the importance of being honest with oneself cannot be overestimated. Many people, indeed most people, try to be honest with themselves, and are as honest as they know how to be. The difficulty many find in their efforts to be honest with themselves lies in the fact that many issues calling for honesty may be buried out of the person's awareness.

When an individual is asked about some information that he has stored in his subconscious, the individual by all rights declares he has no knowledge about such information. "I don't know what you're talking about," he honestly and innocently responds. When a person has been terribly mistreated as a child, whether emotionally or physically, by his or her parents, that person may choose to bury the information in the subconscious and in fact not remember that abuse at all. Along with the denial of the abusive activity, the person will deny the emotions that are associated with it, because they are, by definition, self-depricating emotions. It becomes a struggle for this person to accept information, and to acknowledge the negative feelings and the poor self-attitude, because to do so would necessitate so much unpleasant history to be relived, reassessed, and worked through. The motivation to avoid such a difficult, painful and wearisome task is obvious. However, the importance of the effort and the need to undertake the activity cannot be overestimated. Misunderstood or denied emotions that affect our behavior and attitudes cannot be dealt with until they are understood for what they are.

"Misunderstood or denied emotions that affect our behavior and attitudes cannot be dealth with until they are understood for what they are."

Still waters run deep, and may not reflect treacherous currents and dangerous sandbars. So it is with the reservoir we call the subconscious mind. We must be prepared to painstakingly chart those waters—to investigate that reservoir, and cleanse it of emotions and information that continues to affect our self-perception. We must learn to be master navigators. We must be prepared to undertake a potentially difficult and painful journey, not just through our conscious mind, but through our subconscious mind as well.

Your Values Do Shape Your Behavior

Many psychologists agree that a basic law governs human behavior: activities that are rewarded are generally repeated; whereas, activities that are either ignored or punished are terminated, or at least reduced in frequency.

Behavior that is rewarded may not only continue, but may increase in frequency, increase in intensity, or be modified in other ways in order to strengthen or increase the reward.

The relationship between self-esteem and behavior essentially rests in the nature of reward. Many people think of reward as being monetary, or some other tangible symbol representing a job well done. Indeed, there are behaviorists within psychology who subscribe to the theory that all human behavior is seen as far less independently motivated than it is reactive to given situations.

Such explanation leaves much to be desired, as it tends to deny the individual's ability to will his or her own behavior. These behaviorists' rather robot-like concept of mankind suggests severe limitations on individual free will.

It is my contention, based on extensive research and personal observation, and within the bounds of humanistic and psychodynamic thought, that human beings are self-directed.

While there is no doubt that many of our decisions and actions are influenced greatly by environmental situations and people around us, we do choose our actions from among the choices we recognize.

Often we find ourselves in situations in which we seem to act without even thinking. These situations may be unusual emergencies or situations we've experienced before, but because of previous experiences or an existing conscious awareness, we have already predetermined how we will behave. Although these situations may appear to be examples of reactive behavior, our actions in fact have been well considered, either before the event occured, or during the time in which it occurred, at a conscious or subconscious level. You might look at this as *turning skills into instincts.*

Consider the person who has been trained in first aid, who comes upon an accident scene. Because the training has caused a consciousness of exactly what to do in such a situation, the person moves quickly and efficiently, without having to stop and analyze actions and procedures. This person seems to be acting automatically, when in truth he or she is acting according to a prearranged plan.

Do you remember before you learned how to drive an automobile? It may as well have been a spaceship as it was all so complex. Then, as you were learning, for a time every action was very conscious and deliberate—foot off the accelerator, depress the clutch, shift the gear . . . or signal your intention to change lanes, check the rear view mirror, look over your shoulder, etc., etc. After time, these maneuvers are made with very little conscious thought. In fact, it sometimes becomes a problem because our minds wander so easily while we're driving that we have to consciously focus on the task to avoid carelessness or negligence.

That's the whole theory of practicing any behavior. A pro baseball outfielder knows consciously exactly how to field a fly and throw to the appropriate base. Yet he practices every day throughout the season, programming in every conceivable eventuality he may encounter in a game, because all potentially required action must become second nature to him; he must perform all required movements subconsciously, because conscious thought requires too much time and decision-making, and would probably cost runs. Relying on conscious thought to prompt his actions, our ballplayer wouldn't last in the big leagues for long.

"The subconscious is forever active, guiding our choices regarding our attitudes and our behavior."

The subconscious is forever active, guiding our choices regarding our attitudes and our behavior.

In situations that are either new to us or in some way evoke an array of different choices of actions or behavior, we do weigh our decisions prior to taking action. Often we'll "sleep on it," so our analysis will seem complete, and our decision appear correct. The conscious thought that we give to our actions may be well considered, ill considered, or in some way inadequately considered, but it is considered nonetheless. We are most often aware of our thoughts in new situations.

We base all of our choices concerning our behavior on a comparative basis. We ask ourselves, given this specific behavior or action, what are the most likely consequences? Based on our assessment of those consequences, whether they are likely to be rewarding or nonrewarding to us, we undertake the action considered, or choose an alternative action.

Some might suggest that to this point, our model of human behavior appears as robot-like, or as mechanical, as the behaviorists' response model.

Intrinsic Rewards

The key difference between our model of considered, conscious action, and the behaviorists' response model, lies in the fact that in our model, human beings consider not only external rewards, but intrinsic ones as well.

External rewards are influenced by our values. Some individuals value money more than others, while some value love more than others. Some people will give their all in order to obtain love, whereas others might give their all only to obtain cash.

Our values shape our sense of internal rewards as well.

We will do things, and behave in ways, that enhance our positive feelings about ourselves. People like to feel good about themselves. If we find that our Performance Ratio applied to our performance of a certain task is high, we will find ourselves intrinsically rewarded. If, on the other hand, our performance score is lower than expected, we will feel discouraged about the activity and do our best to avoid similar activities in the future.

At times we are aware of our personal Performance ✗ Ratio. Often we are not. The impact on our self-esteem is experienced either way.

Rewards given to us by others, be it our parents, school officials or our supervisors at work, all serve to enhance our self-esteem. In addition, the rewards we give to ourselves through our positive measures on our Performance Ratio also enhance our self-esteem.

The reward/punishment principle of human behavior, in the context of self-esteem, may thus be restated as: behavior which enchances our self-esteem is likely to be repeated; whereas, behavior which attacks or threatens our self-esteem is likely to be diminished, extinguished and/or avoided.

It is true that this assumes the element of choice. The fact that we can choose from among alternatives in our repertoire enhances the intensity of the feedback. The selection is our responsibility. If someone else chooses for us, we cannot take as much blame for a negative outcome, nor are we able to take much credit when things turn out well.

"Behavior which enhances our self-esteem is likely to be repeated; whereas, behavior which attacks or threatens our self-esteem is likely to be diminished, extinguished and/or avoided."

Often we have no choice over our behavior due to demands of supervisors, parents, etc. and we therefore behave in ways directed by others. In these situations where our self-esteem is enhanced, the positive effect is muted, but there are few problems. But, in situations where our self-esteem is threatened, the potential for personal harm is great. It is these situations in which individuals seek alternatives in order to avoid continuing the behavior that threatens their self-concept. If a way out is found, the self-concept is salvaged. Until that time, the individual feels trapped, powerless and helpless.

It is therefore vital for individuals who have the power to guide, order, and direct the behavior of others, to be sensitive to the issue of the individuals's self-esteem. Through such sensitivity, performance can be enhanced. Through insensitivity, performance will indeed diminish and the individual will experience pain; no one will win.

Given that so many situations do allow for an element of choice, to varying degrees, as we select from our behavioral repertoire, the effect of a behavior which enchances our self-concept appears clear. We are able to feel successful and empowered. However, the relationship between behavior and self-esteem is not a one-way street. Not all of our choices prove successful, and we are never certain of the outcome until after we've made our best choice and gone ahead to complete the behavior.

Element of Risk

Would you walk across a two-by-four suspended six inches above the ground? It's a safe bet most of us would. What if the board is a foot above the ground? Okay, not much of a threat. But what if the board is six feet above the ground? Would you still walk across it? How about if the board is extended between the roofs of two buildings? It's the same board, but with an entirely different risk factor.

Risk-taking is a part of life, but a matter of degree.

It is generally accepted that we do not enjoy, welcome, or seek failure. Any time a behavior or activity is made available to us that allows a significant element of risk, we are threatened. We are threatened with the prospect of failure.

Imagine a 19-year-old fellow we'll call Brian. It's his first year of college, and it's a Friday night. He has no particular girl, so Brian has chosen to check out the action at the local bar. As he sits down, he notices a girl two tables over who appears to be unaccompanied. Brian considers her very attractive and would love to dance with her. Thirty-five minutes and what seemed like buckets of perspiration later, Brian's barstool is empty. He's left alone, dejected and defeated, while the young woman who caught his eye still graces the place two tables over, continuing to enjoy her evening alone. He never tried to approach her.

Brian was afraid of failure. More specifically, he was done in by fear of *rejection*.

Concern about failing may indeed be paralyzing for many of us. Very often people simply choose to not try, in order to avoid failure. Even more common than those who refuse to try at all are the individuals who seek to minimize their losses should they experience failure.

This sounds like a great idea. So how can we reduce or eliminate losses in the case of failure?

We minimize our losses by minimizing our investment in the task at hand.

"How much of our self-esteem are we putting on the line when we choose to try?

Oh, great, you may be saying, now he's becoming a financial advisor ". . . minimizing investment." Don't worry, I'm not referring to investing in the stock market. Our investment here refers to the degree of emotion invested in succeeding at our task. How much of our self-esteem are we putting on the line when we choose to try?

If our 19-year-old friend Brian believes that through a rejection from the attractive young lady he would receive the message that he is worthless and totally unattractive to women, the amount of risk is incredibly high. It is no wonder our friend left the bar without even trying.

Kevin is another 19-year-old sitting at a table near the same attractive young lady in the same bar. Kevin may indeed go over to her with a line like, "Hey, wanna dance?" Although he may be rejected, if Kevin perceives such a rejection as a fact of life, or just something he has to put up with before he goes on to ask the next attractive young lady to dance. "Oh, well, that's the way it goes. Better luck next time," and he shrugs it off. Kevin finds himself in a much better position to cope with the negative feedback that such a rejection provides.

Like so many sales motivators ably convince their audiences, "It's just a numbers game: with each no, you're closer to the yes you're looking for." Many women are familiar with a similar adage, "You have to kiss a lot of frogs to find a prince."

The issue of risk remains a matter of perspective.

Emotional Investment

The message internalized when a rejection is received is essentially the same, regardless of the amount of investment we place in our task. The rejection communicates to us that we are not wanted in the situation, or, in other words, that we have failed in our efforts.

I certainly would in no way suggest that rejection is good news; however, our attitude dictates not only our emotional and behavioral response to the rejection, but also the degree to which we are likely to repeat the behavior. If rejected over some effort in which we have placed a high degree of emotional investment, we are likely to avoid any similar behavior as much as we possibly can. At the least, we will be significantly more intimidated when beginning a similar effort at another time.

Most often, individuals who place a high emotional investment in their success are individuals with very low self-esteem. These people are trying to establish their self-worth through the feedback from their behavior. They are like the gambler who, though he can't afford the loss, goes for broke and bets the farm. They are in need of approval, and seek it outside themselves.

An example of this kind of thinking might be witnessed in a beauty pageant. If a contestant has staked her entire identity on the whim of the judges and winning the crown, and she loses, her self-esteem is severely bruised. But if a contestant is participating for the interesting experience, perhaps for the media exposure, as a lark, or for whatever other reasons, and believes that winning or not winning won't really make much difference in the great stream of life, her self-esteem won't be adversely affected.

It is people with generally high self-esteem who are willing to accept failure as a part of having tried, and consider it an equitable price to pay, at that. These people will still place a significant degree of emotional investment in their effort because they value the activity, but not in order to attain or maintain a positive self-concept. They are more inner-directed in their search for building and maintaining positive self-esteem.

People with high self-esteem, or a relatively positive self-concept, are able to place their emotional investment appropriately in the activity, not in their image of themselves. This is in direct contrast to those with low self-esteem, who tend to place their emotional investment disproportionately in their self-concept. So, when they meet with failure, the effect can be devastating.

"People with high self-esteem are able to place their emotional investment appropriately in the activity, not in their image of themselves."

Sailors

There is, however, an alternative way of approaching life. Given that life is essentially a series of ups and downs (see diagram next page), people who are dependent upon feedback from their behavior in order to validate their self-concept will tend to hedge their bet, and face all aspects of life with minimal emotional investment. They stay at a mid-level, sacrificing the highs to eliminate the lows. We call these people *sailors*. To use an appropriately nautical term, such people have an anchor to windward.

Consider the individual who has invested deeply in several personal relationships. Pattie is just such a lady. In her effort to find warmth and intimacy, Pattie has given her all. For whatever reason, several relationships have not worked out for her. Given the opportunity to enter, once again, into a new relationship, Pattie may find a tendency or temptation to hold back and invest precious little in the relationship. It's an understandable reaction; many of us in similar situations would be similarly cautious with our emotional investment. For some people, however, caution is not enough.

We call these people sailors due to their efforts to sail through life with a minimum of pain. They are often intelligent and very nice people. But because they have been hurt in relationships, because they were hurt in their families as children, or for some unknown reason they don't understand, these people choose to minimize their investment in order to minimize the pain of rejection, failure, or loss.

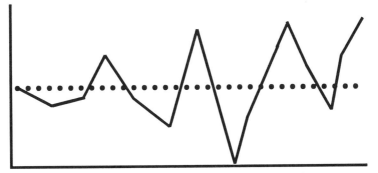

• • • • • indicates the *Sailors*, avoiding the lows of life by sacrificing the highs through <u>controlling</u> their emotional investment.

Consider Peg's situation. Peg was engaged to a wonderful, warm and sensitive man named John. It happened that John was a victim of severe clinical depression. Tragically, before their wedding date, John took his own life. Peg was devastated. She was emotionally drained and thoroughly exhausted. And there was nothing she chould do to change the fact of her loss. For a year and a half following John's death, Peg minimized her involvement with others. She would go to work, do her job, and spend some time with some very close friends.

The devastating loss of John left in its wake a fear in Peg that if she ever loved again, she would risk another tragic ending. Eventually she began venturing out to meet other men, much like one isolated during a terrible storm might hesitantly venture out into the sunshine of a new day. Peg met a wonderful man named Craig about two years after her fiancé John's death. Craig was a kind and generous man with a fun sense of humor. Peg enjoyed this gentleman, and after a time, figured she would marry him. She looked forward to their marriage, but deep in her heart she knew she wasn't enveloped by her love for him, as she had been by her love for John. Peg had become a sailor.

Several months following their marriage, Craig was overheard to say, "I love my wife very much. Peg is dear to me, but, you know, I can only love her so much."

When asked to explain the comment, Craig stated, "Well, as wonderful as she is, and as much as I love her, something may happen. We might get divorced, or she might get sick and die, or get hit by a truck. I might lose her. I'm just not going to accept losing everything, so I'm not going to love her with everything I've got."

Craig, too, was a sailor.

In this actual case history, the marriage of Peg and Craig was basically good, but, as both were sailors, they never reached that ulitmate fulfillment gained by loving fully, completely and unconditionally. It's possible, too, that each subconsciously sensed that the other was holding some-thing back, and not giving the marriage their all.

So, what's wrong with sailing through life? Not a thing. If our goal is to avoid the down-times in life, then by minimizing our investment, we will, at least to a significant degree, succeed. We cannot ignore the negative and un-pleasant situations that we encounter through the proc-esses of living, but we can minimize the impact we have on our self-concept and our lives, through minimizing our emotional investment.

It should be noted that close analysis of the *sailor syndrom* reveals that the preponderance of sailors are men. While definitely not a gender exclusive issue, the sailor attitude or inclination appears highly prevalent in men, and relatively rare in women.

Sir Isaac Newton said, "To every action there is always opposed an equal reaction." As it is in physics, so it is with people: there are consequences—prices we pay—for all our actions. We cannot minimize our investment in order to avoid unpleasant consequences without minimizing or affecting our capacity to enjoy the positive experiences. True, we will still maintain a capacity to enjoy those situations, but that capacity is very restricted.   It is relative to our tightly controlled experience of the unpleasant situations.

> *"We cannot minimize our investment in order to avoid unpleasant consequences without minimizing or affecting our capacity to enjoy the positive experiences."*

I remember hearing a woman once say about her marriage, "The good times are great, the bad times are horrible, but the worst of all are those times that are just mediocre."

The degree to which we allow ourselves to experience the valleys is, in effect, the same degree to which we will allow ourselves to experience the peaks—the positive aspects of our lives.

Choosing Risks

We can see, then, three essential approaches to the process of living. With the first approach, an individual may choose to avoid risks at all costs. This individual is generally one with low self-esteem. While he cannot go through life avoiding all risks, with considerable effort he can enable himself to avoid many or most of the risky situations he encounters. The cost, of course, will be to also avoid pleasure and fulfillment. Brian was not rejected by the girl at the bar, nor did he have a pleasant experience there.

The second approach to life is exemplified by someone who, though not taking unnecessary risks, welcomes risk as an opportunity. Yes, for every risk, there is an element of threat, but these people note the corresponding value of the opportunity in a risky situation. And the person who takes this approach is carful not to place the emotional investment in their self-concept, but, rather, in the activity itself. Perhaps the healthiest perspective to maintain in a risky situation is that, while the threat may be inherent to a situation, so is opportunity.

In order to assist volunteers in a particular fundraising group in Winnipeg, Canada, the group coordinator suggested that while their task was difficult and carried with it a great degree of risk, these volunteers could perhaps view their situation as an "opporthreat." Though the task was initially perceived as overwhelming, the group responded well to this clever point of view. They recognized the inherent threat, yet also saw the commensurate opportunity. Ultimately, the group was successful in their efforts to raise sufficient funds to further their cause.

It's wise to remember that the Chinese pictogram for *crisis* signifies both danger and opportunity.

The third approach to life is embodied by the sailors. Through minimizing his or her investment in relationships and other actions, the sailor enables himself or herself to function with the fears reduced. Pattie was a sailor, and Peg became one, too. Sailors care, they just place very rigid controls over how much they care. They participate in relationships, they just hold back, sacrificing the highs to minimize the lows.

If you control the stakes you bring to the game, you will control, to some extent, the amount you lose, and the pleasure you derive. There can be great excitement in risk-taking. That's what Las Vegas, Atlantic City and Monte Carlo are all about! A lyric line from an old Frankie Laine song of years ago says, "If you haven't gambled for love and lost, then you haven't gambled at all." But certainly, and obviously, if one can't financially, or emotionally, afford the loss, and loses, the excitement quickly turns to pain, and the

". . . behavior consistent with our values will be self-esteem enhancing, whereas behavior that is inconsistent with our values will threaten our self-esteem."

pleasure of the opportunity offers little if any help in combating or counterbalancing that pain. the pain of an ill-afforded loss is not conducive to boosting self-esteem.

The relationship between self-esteem and behavior is, then, an interdependent one. Behavior that enhances our self-esteem is likely to be repeated. Behavior that threatens our self-esteem is likely to be avoided. This implies that behavior consistent with our values will be self-esteem enhancing, and indeed intrinsically rewarding; whereas, behavior that is inconsistent with our values will threaten our self-esteem.

We may find ways to rationalize or in other ways enable ourselves to continue the behavior that threatens our self-concept. However, the general relationship between our behavior and our self-esteem appears clear.

The interdependent notion comes into play in the second consideration discussed above, whereby people with higher self-esteem tend to interject a greater sense of risk into their lives. These folks are better able to cope with risk, because they don't stake their self-concept on the risk. People with low self-esteem will either avoid risk-taking behavior, or seek to control the potential negative messages to their self-concept by minimizing emotional investment.

low self esteem

Low Self-Esteem and Chemical Dependency

Millions of people in America use drugs. Most everyone uses drugs.

People use drugs when prescribed by physicians. People use drugs when they reach for over-the-counter medications such as aspirin for headaches. People use drugs in their daily lives without even being aware of it, such as caffeine in coffee, tea and chocolate.

People also use drugs such as alcohol on a regular basis. And many people use illicit—that is, illegal—drugs on a regular basis. People develop addictions or abuse/dependency problems to these controlled substances.

Does everyone who uses drugs develop an abuse problem? Probably not. Does everyone who uses drugs have an addiction problem? Definitely not.

What is Addiction?

What, then, constitutes drug *abuse* as opposed to drug *use?* Anyone whose use of chemicals causes or contributes significantly to problems in his or her life who continues to use in the face of those problems has a chemical abuse/dependency problem.

When making an assessment as to the presence of a chemical abuse problem, or assessing the extent of such a problem, professionals look at four key areas in a person's life. First, does this person's use of chemicals cause problems with their health? Take for example the individual who goes to the doctor for a check-up and is told that another drink will cause his liver to fail and cause the drinker to die. Such a patient may choose, through his own anxiety upon learning this information, to seek solace through intoxication, and reach for another drink. This individual has an obvious health-related problem connected to his consumption of alcohol.

Another key area a professional would examine to assess a drug problem centers around family relationships. Does this individual's use of alcohol and/or other drugs contribute to problems with his or her spouse, parents, children or anyone else he or she is particularly close to? It is important to consider that just because someone's spouse exhibits significant concern over an individuals's consumption of drugs does not necessarily mean that the person has a problem directly connected to drugs. However, whether it is the individual's problem related to his consumption, or his partner's unrealistic perceptions of the situation, the individual nonetheless has a problem which needs investigation. Most often, when someone complains about the chemical habits of someone close to them, a drug-related problem does exist.

The third key area to consider is legality. An individual who repeatedly gets arrested for drunk driving or drug-related disturbances, has a definite problem. While many clients have suggested to me that their problem lies more with a judge's intolerance of their consumption of alcohol or other drugs, further investigation bears out the fact that their consumption is indeed their own problem.

The fourth key area to consider in assessing an individual's potential for problems with drugs is the use of drugs in the workplace. Does the individual's consumption interfere with his productivity? Does it contribute to absenteeism? Is he having difficulty holding onto the job because of his consumption of chemicals?

"Our society tends to operate with different or confusing values when it comes to the issue of alcohol and other drugs."

These are questions that serve to determine whether an individual is having problems with drug consumption or not.

A word of caution: Our society tends to operate with different or confusing values when it comes to the issue of alcohol and other drugs. While almost everyone would agree that the number one drug problem in North America is alcohol, the news media, health professionals, and lay people often refer to "alcohol and drugs." This reference strongly suggests that alcohol is something other than a drug. Alcohol is indeed a drug. When the term "drugs" is utilized in this book, it shall refer to all drugs—alcohol, illicit drugs, and legal drugs, be they over-the-counter or prescribed by a medical doctor. An individual may manifest problems in any of the four areas of life noted above with any single drug, or with a combination of drugs.

Why do people use drugs? For a variety of reasons. People use drugs to medicate, some use drugs to relax, some to be social, and on and on. There are ostensibly as many reasons as there are people who use.

Drug Abuse

The difference between using and abusing drugs is found quite directly in the definition of drug abuse. When the use causes problems, the use becomes abuse. In order for drug use to become drug dependency, or chemical dependency, abuse must exist. The individual who continues to use the chemical in the face of problems is abusing the substance. Whether this use is accomplished and maintained through the operation of defense mechanisms such as denial (see Chapter Two) is not necessarily relevant.

There is an additional level of drug abuse that is found when an individual becomes habituated to his or her drug of choice. This level is generally referred to as dependency, i.e., the individual places a supreme importance on that drug, and the drug becomes more important to the individual than anything else in that person's life. Superceding all else, the drug becomes "Number One."

In dependency, the addiction becomes physical. Physically dependent individuals do not seek to use the drug, generally, to get high or to relax. Rather, they have developed a need for the drug in order to feel "normal." They need the drug in order to function. They need their drug in order to get up in the morning, or to go to work, or to present their sales plan in front of their colleagues, or to communicate with their spouses or families. When such a situation exists, there are usually two markers generally accepted in chemical dependency treatment circles to indicate chemical dependency.

The initial issue considered is whether or not there has been an increase in tolerance. An increase in tolerance occurs simply when it takes more of the same drug to achieve the same degree of "high." As one's body becomes used to the particular drug, the body habituates itself to the drug, and finds that without increasing amounts, it doesn't feel right. The person just doesn't feel right.

The second marker in drug dependency is the presence of withdrawal symptoms in the absence of the drug. Once a body has become habituated, the withdrawal may be either psychological or physical, or both. In the case of alcohol, there is a specific set of symptoms that an individual who is physically dependent on the drug goes through when in withdrawal. These symptoms are specifically called the *delirium tremens*, or DTs. The DTs may include the shakes, tingling in the arms and legs, difficulty in walking, difficulty in balance, hallucinations and/or delusions, and so on. Other drugs may also yield specific withdrawal symptoms when the drug is voluntarily or involuntarily withheld.

What is the relationship between drug use or abuse and self-esteem?

Chemical Anesthetic

/

One way to answer that question is to consider the young man who, at the age of 19, goes into a bar. Yes, you remember our young friend Brian. He's still seeking a relationship with a special young lady. He sees that very attractive lady two tables over, and he is reluctant to ask her to dance. Brian consumes several bottles of beer (or does several lines of cocaine, or whatever drug he prefers), gets up from his chair, and approaches the lady. She responds affirmatively or negatively.

What's the difference to the scenario laid out in the previous chapter? Brian did not have the courage to approach her without alcohol in his system. After several drinks, he does approach her. What is the qualitative difference?

Taking a "shot of courage" is a woefully common expression. Many alcoholism treatment professionals and self-help groups speak in terms of "bottled courage"—a chemically induced bravado. Has this young man drunk some courage in order to approach this lady? Did he find his courage at the bottom of a bottle?

Fact: The consumption of chemicals does not add anything to an individual's character, personality, lifestyle, nor life in general. No one can find social skills or personality traits in a bottle, a baggie, or a pill case.

While drugs do not add anything to an individual's life or lifestyle, drugs may very well take away the pain of not being the person one wants to be. Drugs may take away any pain.

"The consumption of chemicals does not add to an individual's character, personality, life, or lifestyle. No one can find social skills or personality traits in a bottle, a baggie, or a pill case."

Drugs do indeed have a mental, and even a physical, numbing effect. In Brian's case, he no longer worried about the possible rejection. He didn't care. His ability to cope with rejection was enhanced, not through additional skill-building and confidence, but through a sense of numbness, a dulling effect. If he were rejected, the pain of the rejection would just roll right off, and Brian would be likely to approach another woman, and another.

What, then, is the problem? Isn't such "gutsiness," or determination, good?

Psychologist, author and social critic Stanton Peele developed a model to discuss the relationship between chemical consumption and self-esteem. Dr. Peele would consider our friend Brian to be an individual with low self-esteem. As such, he would have a stong reluctance to approach the attractive woman due to his perceived inability to handle the rejection he would expect.

Brian consumes a drug, effectively numbing himself, and goes along his merry way. In Dr. Peele's model, our friend cannot help but consider his activities the next day. While he may remember with satisfaction that he danced with the young lady (a victory!) and perhaps had a generally rousing good time, he cannot fail to note that he could approach the young lady only through the assistance of chemical consumption. In sports terminology, his "victory" would have a very large asterisk, like a wind-aided long jump. And in his heart of hearts, he'd know the victory was a hollow one.

In Dr. Peele's model, the individual is left with a hollow, sinking feeling that, left to his own devices, relying on his own native ingenuity and charm, he would not have been able to make such an approach. As a result, he accepts the need for the crutch in his life. But that acceptance carries a price. He's knocked down a level or two in his own eyes. His self-esteem is lowered.

"With self-esteem lowered even more through chemical consumption, the need for continued chemical consumption in order to elevate self-esteem, albeit artificially, becomes more pressing."

With his self-esteem lowered even more through his chemical consumption, the need for continued chemical consumption in order to elevate, albeit artificially, his self-esteem, becomes more pressing. As the self-esteem goes down, the need for chemical consumption goes up, as the need for chemical support goes up, the individual's perception of his self-esteem goes down.

This cycle continues until the chemical use becomes habitual, and leads to systematic abuse and/or dependency.

This model may require additional research; however, I concur—based upon my work with thousands of individuals with chemical dependency-related problems—that it is impossible to ignore the obvious fact: while the nature of chemical dependency problems differ significantly from person to person, the common denominator is low self-esteem. By the time individuals present themselves for treatment, their self-esteem has eroded significantly. At this point, many will acknowledge that it becomes more and more difficult to face themselves in the mirror. Their dependency on their particular drug or drugs of choice has left them with a very unpleasant self-image.

Systematic Suicide

An additional concept related to the issue of chemical consumption comes from psychologist Lee Silverstein. Dr. Silverstein presents the notion of *systematic suicide*.

Dr. Silverstein asks the logical question, "How can you continue to consume chemicals when you know that such consumption is harmful to you?"

Consider the issue of cigarettes. We have all been educated over the last 20 to 30 years about the very real potential for harm to nicotine users. While many individuals have quit smoking because of this information, millions continue to smoke, and to start the cigarette habit, despite knowledge of this information.

Many long-term smokers acknowledge the potential harm, and say that if they had known the facts, they would have never started smoking. But they continue to smoke. It is difficult to defend the point that, just because cigarette smoking is a physical addiction and difficult to quit, these people are still smoking in the face of such overwhelming evidence of its dangers. And what is amazing, even heart-breaking, is, many of these people have children who have learned the evils of the cigarette habit in elementary school, and who plead with their parents to quit, even going so far as to cut their parents cigarettes in half in their attempt to lessen the amount the parent smokes. And still the parent continues smoking.

Quitting smoking may not be easy, but it can be done. Continuing the habit defies all logic. Dr. Silverstein strongly suggests through his model that there are only two reasons to continue using drugs in the face of unequivocal proof that such use is physically dangerous. One is sheer stupidity. The other is an attempt to kill oneself.

If one is attempting to kill himself or herself, there are many, many ways to do the deed. But suicide is against the most basic human instincts. Most of us choose to live . . . to avoid killing ourselves. But self-abuse is another story. Due to a very low self-concept, many individuals may choose to cause harm to themselves as a punishment.

The issue of self-abuse and self-defeating behavior such as drug consumption, which the person is aware of as being physically harmful or even life-threatening, is a large issue occupying much psychological research and psychological theory.

An extension of Dr. Silverstein's basic theory of systematic suicide leads us to conclude that childhood trauma which leaves low self-esteem in its wake, or an on-going low-grade Performance Ratio, or any external input that diminishes our self-concept, will yield self-defeating behavior. Does that mean that this self-defeating behavior is intentional?

In some cases, it may be. But in most cases, people do not consciously say, "Boy, I really hate myself. Pass me a pack of cigarettes so that I can punish myself for being the rotten kind of person I am." However, subconsciously holding onto the idea that one is an unworthy person may yield self-sabotaging behavior. It may be that, due to the subconsciously held belief of unworthiness, individuals choose chemicals and/or other self-defeating behaviors (eating disorders, inappropriate choices for intimate relationships, and so on) in order to punish themselves—to knock themselves down to the low level at which they see themselves.

If Dr. Silverstein's model is applied universally, it would posit that all people who smoke or use other drugs in the face of the knowledge of specific and undeniable danger to them, are either stupid or out to kill themselves in a slow, progressive and systematic manner. While I support the concept of systematic suicide as a possible explanation for some self-defeating behaviors, one needs to consider, once again, the discussion of the subconscious and how powerful that subconscious is.

Drugs and Risk

While we are very much aware of the potential dangers of cigarettes and other drugs we consume, the concept of harm actually befalling us personally is deferred through mechanisms known as defenses. We use the mechanism of denial to say, "It won't happen to me."

The issue of "not me-denial" is easily illustrated as follows. Hypothetically, say it is generally accepted that nine out of every ten smokers will die from emphysema or lung cancer. In the face of such statistics, were they accurate, the individual smoker would walk into a room with nine other smokers and say, "I'm sorry to hear about your tragedy, but it just won't happen to me. I'm the one out of ten."

"Does this mean that people who use drugs are indeed strong, confident, even cocky risk takers, and therefore have healthy, positive self-esteem?"

Does this mean that people who use drugs are indeed strong, confident, even cocky risk takers, and therefore have healthy, positive self-esteem?

In some cases an arguement can be made that people with a healthy sense of self-esteem acknowledge the risks, weigh them both ways, and choose to take the risks, considering them warranted, or justified. Is a ninety-percent chance of contracting lung cancer or other serious consequences as the result of cigarette smoking a warranted or justified risk? If the consumption of cigarettes is truly that important to the individual, perhaps he or she would be able to rationalize that the risk is justified. This is truly an individual choice; however, the general societal wisdom would lead us in a direction of avoiding cigarette smoking. It is denial—"it won't happen to me"—at a conscious or subconscious level which tends to keep most drug abusers consuming drugs.

Perhaps a word is in order about a concept common to youth: presumed immortality. The capacity of rationalization that "that just happens to older people; kids don't die of diseases" is particularly profound in younger people. A prime example is the mass of evidence that skin cancer is killing at an increasing rate; moreover, there is scientific proof that cancer-causing ultraviolet rays are accumulated in the body, much like radiation, and that high accumulations in the teen years aren't reflected in diagnoses of cancer until decades later. Nonetheless, on any beach in the world, it's common to find young people (admittedly joined by some older people) boldly basking in the sun, with no mind to obstructing their bronze tans with sunscreens.

Government statistics also reveal an alarming rise in teen smoking, presumably encouraged by the prevalent youthful denial, "kids don't get lung cancer." True: the damage doesn't manifest itself in the form of lung cancer until the kids—having continued the smoking habit—are in their forties, fifties or older.

Emotional Stagnation

An additional aspect of chemical use and chemical abuse has to do with the concept of numbing not only pain, but numbing emotions in general. It is widely accepted in the field of chemical dependency that chemical use retards, or at the very least stunts, emotional growth. We endeavor through our chemical use to control our emotional responses to various situations in our lives. While we may not be able to predict the future and foresee what situations are likely to come up in our lives, if we medicate ourselves though chemical use, we can attempt to place controls over our emotional responses to unpredictable situations. In other words, the drugs can keep us at that safe mid-level occupied by the *sailors* of Chapter Three. Drugs conveniently create the bounds of our emotions, protecting us from depressing lows while preventing the elating natural highs. We become sailors on seas of chemicals.

While this effort to control our responses may sound somewhat healthy for those who have difficulty controlling their emotions without chemicals, the issue here is found in the cost of that control. In order to control emotional responses through chemical use, people deny themselves the opportunity to learn. When we control our emotional responses through chemical use, we restrict our capacity to observe and experience and learn and grow.

We cannot respect our *selves* when we make choices that serve to suppress or deny our feelings, whether the choices involve the use of chemicals, or the assumption of some other personal restriction of whatever sort. When we use chemicals to block or limit natural emotions, we consciously or subconsciously generate and experience frustration. The frustration provokes anger. We then direct that anger inward, where it can fester and grow.

Chemical abuse limits personal development and growth; therefore, it progressively erodes self-esteem. Artificially controlling emotions usually results in avoidance: avoidance of conflict, avoidance of commitment, avoidance of change, and avoidance of growth.

> *"Chemical abuse limits personal development and growth, and progressively erodes self-esteem."*

We do not avoid feeling the way we feel through chemical use, we simply *mask* those feelings, making it difficult or impossible to acknowledge, understand, accept or change those feelings.

Your *Inside* You: Core Self-Image

Self-esteem is the root of human existence. Our self-esteem is our honest, unadorned, unadulterated view of our selves, our worth, our importance. We draw this view from the totality of our experiences through life, and filter it through our own filtering system. It is likened to a personal, private and intangible photo album of ourselves, compiled throughout our lives. These pictures of ourselves that we carry in our minds significantly influence all phases of our lives—our attitudes and behaviors, our relationships with others, our careers, our families, our goals and ambitions, our wants and our fears, our values.

Values are our personal set of standards, or principles, which we maintain consistent with our belief system. People will say, "I can't do that; it's against my conscience," or, "I've got to follow my conscience." *Conscience* is typically what we call our system of values. Conscience is defined in Webster's Seventh New Collegiate Dictionary as "the sense or consciousness of the moral goodness or blameworthiness of one's own conduct, intentions or character together with a feeling of obligation to do right or be good."

We all have a picture of ourselves. That picture may be more positive than negative, more negative than positive, or somewhere in the middle. There is no one in the world who has no self-esteem. It's impossible for any living, breathing human being to be without it.

"There is no one in the world who has no self-esteem. It's impossible for any living, breathing human being to be without it."

There are many of us who from time to time experience what appears to be a void of self-esteem—a complete lacking. But, no, the self-esteem is there; it's just very low, perhaps nearly "off the scale." The principle is similar to a photograph: one end of the spectrum is a sharp print, high in contrast. That's like high, positive self-esteem. The other end of the spectrum is a film negative, which is like low self esteem. But the image of the photograph is still there, whichever end of the spectrum you examine. So self-esteem is always there, whether it's high or low.

Every moment of every day, each of us maintains a picture of ourselves, a sense of who we are. It may be an exciting, wonderful photographic portrait, like a Richard Avedon or Annie Liebowicz, or horrible, like your DMV or passport photo. But we always have a self-picture. We always have self-esteem, positive or negative.

How then does one achieve **positive self-esteem** and **strong personal values?**

"State vs Trait" Self-Esteem

It is best to consider the issue of self-esteem as a *process* rather than a state of being. At any given time during the process of achieving consistently high self-esteem, one may have low self-esteem, high self-esteem, or be somewhere in between. The level of self-esteem fluctuates. It fluctuates a little in response to changes in our environment, and it fluctuates over time. So our picture of our self changes as the input we receive changes.

While it is true that most people have different self-images in different situations, as we discuss below, we are more concerned here about a person's lasting image, his or her **trait** self-image, rather than his or her self-concept which responds to environmental, or external, occurrences all around us.

I may see myself as a very competent trainer, and a highly skilled clinician. When working in a clinical or training environment, my self-picture is pretty solid, my personal self-esteem rating pretty high. I may see myself as a moderately competent tennis player and as such, when on the tennis court, my self-image rating is probably medium. Now, given the opportunity to score a difficult point, in that moment, my self-image rating may go up. Following a missed return or a relatively easy shot fluffed, my self-image would go down.

In spite of my feeling good about my professional skills, and even pretty good about my weekend tennis game, I see myself as a totally incompetent brain surgeon. I therefore would wholeheartedly recommend against anyone agreeing to such surgery if I were to perform it. Picturing myself in an operating theater with the appropriate tools and the best surgical support staff in medical history, about to commence brain surgery, would cause my self-picture to nosedive. My self-concept at that time would be very low. It would be low due to my horrible expectations. In that setting I would expect to be a hopeless incompetent.

"The fluctuations in one's self-esteem in response to all that happens around us are a normal part of living."

The fluctuations in one's self-image in response to all

that happens around us are a normal part of living. They reflect the fact that we live in a complex, dynamic and constantly changing world. And, paired with the fact that each individual is a complex, dynamic and constantly changing being, we have every reason to expect modifications in our self-pictures, our self-concepts, all along the road of life.

These modifications are *adjustments to the core*. The core self-image is the essential picture of ourselves that we carry constantly. These pictures are essentially resistant to change. Sure, we do modify the pictures based on new information. We modify the picture based on our successive Performance Ratio scores and we modify the overall self-image based on external input as well. These modifications are seldom more than minor modifications to the overall core. It's like simply wearing different clothes; our face and body remain the same.

As we look at our self-esteem in a variety of different situations—often referred to as situational self-esteem—we are more concerned with how we feel about ourselves in any given set of circumstances. Our self-image will change, perhaps even drastically, from circumstance to circumstance, just as my self-image fluctuates when I see myself as a teacher, tennis player, and brain surgeon. Perhaps we see ourselves as a more practiced and therefore more effective husband or wife rather than parent, and, as such, find our self-picture to be much more pleasant when we see ourselves in the spousal role rather than in the parental role.

> *"Although somewhat responsive to environmental contingencies, the core self-image is relatively unchanging through time and through the course of the events of our lives."*

Our core self-image, often referred to as trait self-esteem, is the *characteristic* way in which we think and feel about ourselves. Although somewhat responsive to environmental contingencies, the core self-image is relatively unchanging through time and through the course of the events of our lives.

What then is the relationship between trait self-esteem and situational self-esteem? For the sake of clarity, let's consider them as analogous to a building: trait self-esteem is the foundation, and situational self-esteem is the portion of the structure most often undergoing remodelling. The remodelling builds upon the core structure and serves to modify the overall building, but the foundation remains the same—unless the remodelling is such that the foundation is threatened, or, as part of a massive remodelling project, is also enhanced.

Although trait self-esteem is relatively constant and resistant to change, the relationship between trait and situational self-esteem lies in what kind of feedback we receive from different situations we experience, and how the feedback influences us. Those of us who tend toward a relatively low trait self-esteem would have very, very few situations in which our situational self-esteem would be significantly higher. Conversely, those of us with high trait self-esteem would find very few situations in which environmental factors would serve to lower our situational self-esteem significantly.

The degree of the effect of situations yielding low self-esteem, and the duration the effect is felt, is moderated by our trait esteem. High trait self-esteem will minimize such impact, while low trait self-esteem would tend to magnify the experience.

In all honesty, my example of finding myself in an operating theater with the tools and support staff to perform brain surgery, while illustrative, is really virtually impossible for someone with my background and training. It is much more common for people to find themselves in situations which pretty much correlate with their background, interests, and skills. Indeed, individuals naturally seek to be involved in environments which are consistent with their characteristic self-picture. As one who sees very clearly that he would be a less-than-competent brain surgeon, I will never seek to be scrubbed and dressed in green gown and surgical mask as head of a neurological surgical team. And, candidly speaking, recognizing my limited skills on the tennis court, I have yet to invite Stefan Edberg or Jimmy Connors to a match.

The issue of core self-image, and the distinction between trait and situational self-esteem, is similar to the concept of trait or situational anxiety. While all of us are more anxious in some circumstances than others, we have a certain characteristic level of anxiety. Our characteristic level of anxiety, or trait anxiety, suggests how prone we are to feeling anxious across the broad spectrum of situations we may encounter. And it is true that, even though our trait anxiety can be very low, that is to say we're not easily ruffled or nervous, our situational anxiety can be very keen.

The best example of an almost universally anxiety-provoking situation is public speaking. It's said to be one of the most wrenching fears known to man—even exceeding fear of death for many people. There are many extremely accomplished and highly regarded people for whom public speaking is a major white-knuckler. However, because their trait anxiety is low, and their core self-image is high, they learn how to "feel the fear and do it anyway," to borrow the title of the Susan Jeffers book (see Bibliography). Or, more specifically, "they have the butterflies, but they've learned to make them fly in formation." [In the spirit of building successes into our lives as a general self-esteem enhancer and all-around self-improvement tool, we would be remiss not to mention here an organization called Toastmasters International, headquartered in Santa Ana, California. It has ably assisted hundreds of thousands of people all over the world to improve public speaking skills, and, in the process, gain substantial poise and markedly improved self-esteem.]

While our level of self-esteem in specific situations is important, the importance is limited to our performance, attitudes, and emotions in those exact situations. Our trait self-esteem, or core self-image, remains quite steady across situations—unless we take considerable concentrated effort to change.

Our core self-image is powerful in its resistance to change and in its effect on our behavior and feelings. Where the specifics of a situation may effect us, our core self-image is like a rock. When it is positive, it offers us protection and relative consistency. When it is negative, we have little refuge from the stormy times of life. We are most concerned with our core self-image

". . . our core self-image is like a rock. When it is positive, it offers us protection and relative consistency. When it is negative, we have little refuge from the stormy times of life."

as we seek to enhance our self-worth and maintain strong personal values and positive self-esteem.

The relationship between our trait self-esteem and the goals we set, the risks we take, and our entire pattern of growth, is a significant and solid one. Our characteristic self-picture serves as a guide for behaviors we choose to undertake.

The world of our experiences is not under our complete control. From time to time, we find ourselves in situations that do not coexist well with our trait self-esteem. These are risky situations, and opportunities for growth.

Because these situations provide opportunities for growth, they are important; however, our trait self-esteem must be reliably strong to empower us to actively seek opportunities to increase our characteristic self-picture. We can view these situations or opportunities around us as stepping stones, but we must be sure our footing is solid before we tread upon them. High trait self-esteem affords us the solid footing we need.

As we increase our trait self-esteem, we naturally increase our ability to surmount situations that challenge our self-picture and, in turn, we grow even stronger.

Keys to Strong Personal Values and Positive Self-Esteem

People who feel out of control, powerless, hopeless, and helpless feel as though there is nothing inside them. Most of us can identify with that feeling; even if just momentarily, from time to time, most human beings have felt as though they have no self-esteem at all.

There is no such thing as the absence of self-esteem.

In times of despair, our self-esteem is very low. Yet, even when beaten down by a troubled view of ourselves or of events around us—whether an accurate reflection of reality or not—we still retain a self-picture, and therefore a foundation upon which to build back up to a more positive self-concept.

Following are **Seven Keys** for you to use to build and maintain a position of strong personal values and positive self-esteem.

Self-Assessment: A Realistic Approach

The **First Key** addresses the logical first stage in the development of your positive self-image: **Take a realistic**

self-inventory.

We need to see just where we are, where we want to go, and what about us will aid us in getting there. So we must take an honest look at our strengths and our shortcomings. We all have both. We all have things in which we excell, and things in which we don't do so well.

The realistic self-inventory is a three-step process.

Step one is to take a sheet of paper and divide it into two columns. At the top of one column, write "Strengths" and at the top of the other "Limitations." List as many items as possible which honestly belong in one column or the other.

There is no need to attempt a balance between the columns, and there are no right or wrong answers. All that is called for is honest responses. In the initial step of this process, our goal is simply to familiarize ourselves with the things we think we do well, the skills or assets we possess, and the things we don't do well, or our relative weaknesses.

In step two, the process undergoes a little refinement. Next to each of the items listed, we need to identify whether these traits can be changed, or whether they are beyond our capacity to modify. Traits we hope to change merit an asterisk (*), indicating that we *can* change those particular traits, and will work to do so. For example, under "Strengths," we may see ourselves as patient—as patient as we want ourselves to be. We may also acknowledge our sense of honesty, but admit we would like to be be even moreso. We would place an asterisk next to "honesty" on our list, but leave "patient" unmarked. And in the "Limitations" column, we may list lack of assertiveness and, because our life's goal is to play in the NBA and we're 5'4", height. Assertiveness gets an asterisk, because we can obtain assertiveness training and improve our skills. But there's nothing we can do to overcome our height limitation.

In step three of the process, we identify a friend or family member we trust implicitly, with whom we can review our list. While it is true that we are often our own worst critic, we are occasionally overly kind or a little blind in certain areas. Even in our most sincere efforts to be honest, issues such as defense mechanisms, outside pressures, and demands or wishes of others can cloud the picture and prevent complete accuracy.

If it is difficult to find someone in your life who you trust to be completely objective about the items on your self inventory, don't despair. This issue can be handled in one of two ways. The first way is to consult with different friends concerning different items on our list with which they would have specific knowledge or experience, and obtain a "reality check" from our closest friend or significant other only on the items we have complete confidence they'll be able to be straight-forward and forthcoming about.

Often, because of the complexities of relationships, we may not feel that anyone we know will be one hundred percent objective. It would certainly be best to avoid baring such personal information in a situation which is less than ideal. No one needs that potential aggravation. As an alternative to going to friends and loved ones, approaching a member of the clergy, a pastoral counselor or a professional therapist is appropriate for step three. These individuals can generally be completely trusted to be constructive and supportive as they apply their professional skills to assist in your efforts to adequately identify the strengths and limitations on your self-inventory.

"Just as our self-picture changes over time and through innumerable events and experiences, so do our strengths and our limitations."

Once these three steps have been completed, you will have a realistic self-inventory. But this is not the end of the process.

Just as our self-picture changes over time and through the innumerable events and experiences of life, so do our strengths and our limitations. Your realistic self-inventory must be constantly reviewed on whatever schedule that feels appropriate for you, but not less than annually, and, in the face of considerable change in your life, more frequently. It is often helpful to enlist that trusted second opinion on the realistic self inventory reviews as well as in its initial development.

Values are Vital

Earlier we discussed the issue of values. What are values? Values are issues that are important to us as individuals. Values are, generally speaking, items of principle which we maintain consistent with our beliefs. Values embraced by many in our society include money, power, love, security, family, self-esteem, education, physical health, honesty, justice, and many others. Values are interrelated with your system of ethics.

The First Key to a positive self-esteem is a realistic self-inventory; the **Second Key: Be true to your personal values.**

First, we need to assess our values, understand them, and determine their degree of fit in our lives. In addition to understanding our values, there is a necessity to gain some sense of understanding as to where they originated.

Values do come from all of the external influences we talked about in Chapter One—the same influences which tend to give us our self-concept. Values are constantly tested by our ongoing experience, and by our judgment of that experience over time. Through the process of education, and the general nature of change, our values are often modified, sometimes discarded, and often enhanced or strengthened.

The first stage in values development is exposure. Being

exposed to ideas or beliefs of others is only an opportunity to adopt their concepts into your own system—your personal code of ethics. If exposed to values through religious involvement and / or through parents, significant others, or some other respected source, such involvement and experience will have an enhanced impact once the values are put through the individual's internalizing process.

One needs to play with one's values . . . to determine one's level of comfort with them. They cannot feel comfortable if they are not your own. Values which don't fit are the "shoulds"—the things you don't really subscribe to deep down inside, but which keep coming up in your thinking because they are supposed to fit—probably by someone else's standards. But they don't fit. If the values don't fit, it doesn't mean they're bad or wrong. They're just not yours.

The second stage in values development is that internalizing process mentioned above, to separate those values that fit from those that do not. This process hinges on understanding the context—are these values idealistic? Am I motivated to accept them as my own because I want to please someone else? Do they fit for me at this time, at this particular stage of my life?

Some values will fit into your personal code; accept them. Some will fail to meet your criteria; discard them. Others may land in between; you'll find them as partially or sometimes fitting. These values offer guidelines, but are relatively flexible and adaptable.

The values that fit comfortably, consistently and lastingly are your *core values*. There is no question as to their ongoing importance to you. Those that seem not quite so perfect a fit may be less important and constitute values that come more into play with specific circumstances.

The third stage in developing your system of values, or code of ethics, revolves around the hierarchial arrangement of your values. Those that apply in all phases of your life are primary, or core values; those that partially fit may dominate in particular situations, but as a general rule they would be secondary values. However, all values, core or secondary, must be prioritized. You must rank them in order of their importance to the way you live.

Why are values important at all? Values act as your personal guide for living. Now, this is not a guide checked out of the library, purchased at a bookstore, or out of the racks at the grocery store checkout counter. The guide is your own creation, for your own use. You should view it as bound in leather, with your name embossed in gold on the cover—your own personal bible, of you, for you. This is implicitly right, because if a personal system of values is to be effective, it must be entirely and exclusively your own.

> *"If a personal system of values is to be effective, it must be entirely and exclusively your own."*

The guide does not provide a complete step-by-step approach to life. At least that should not be the intention of your set of values. The purpose of the guide is to establish parameters that enable one to judge one's own behavior, and to offer standards by which behavior can be accepted, rejected or modified. These parameters, these guideposts, are core values.

Core values are not situational. Core values are valid in all situations, crisscrossing through all phases of your life. Your core values guide you equally through all situations—any one particular value serving in all situations of a particular nature, as opposed to being situation-specific. For example, the value of respecting personal property doesn't stop at money, or automobiles, or jewelry, but covers anything a person is capable of owning. If one believes in—or values—the concept of fidelity, would one avoid sleeping with the neighbor's wife, but go ahead and sleep with the wife of the gentleman across the street? Of course not, because such behavior would be inconsistent with one's established core values.

The serious consequence of inconsistency with one's own values is a very negative personal message. That message is that even though I set my own standards, I cannot achieve those standards nor maintain them.

The power of that message, the negative power, and the resulting assault on one's self-esteem, comes not only from the knowledge that the standards were self-selected and self-built, but also from the knowledge that the assessment is self-generated. The judgment comes from within the one who committed the deed, the one who missed the mark. It is not your Mom saying you didn't live up to what she told you to do; nor is it your Dad saying you failed to do as he taught you.

". . . we rate our behaviors, our thoughts, our feelings, our attitudes, and our actions according to the degree of fit between them and our system of core values."

Just as we give scores to our behavior (Performance Ratio), we rate our behaviors, our thoughts, our feelings, our attitudes, and our actions according to the degree of fit we find between them and our system of core values.

For those components of our personal code of ethics that aren't so broad in scope, so universal and comprehensive— the secondary values—we tend to allow ourselves considerable leeway in our efforts to live up to them. We are less stringent with them than we are with those primary core values which we hold more closely.

There are a number of temptations to challenge our efforts to live by our personal code. We do stray from our chosen path from time to time. Our environment is just too complex to expect otherwise. We face conflicts in our system of values all the time.

Should we return that money we found, or donate it to

the poor, or spend it on our own needs? Should we work longer and harder at our jobs to get that promotion, or should we work less and spend more time with our family?

Each choice refelcts a value. Faced with conflicts in values, our personal code of ethics offers help—but the choice is seldom black and white. Within those shades of gray offered by selecting one choice over another, we must create and foster an allowance of tolerance. We cannot satisfy all of our values all of the time.

Even among our highest ranked core values, we need to tolerate some variance, as no path of guidance should be too rigid to disallow some movement or flexibility. Most people value truth; however, it's difficult to imagine any adult human being who hasn't told a tiny, harmless little lie which saved him, or someone else, from a greater assault on a personal system of values. In full acknowledgement of the importrance of flexibility in our efforts to adhere to our values, the second Key to a positive self-esteem, is achieved through **being true to your values.**

In our effort to make it through a complex array of choices and consequences which create the drama of life, it is essential to talk things over with valued friends and confidants, to seek help, and to allow help to be provided.

We Need to Develop and Maintain a System of Support

Unlike many other systems, your personal support system is composed of people and places. Each of us has places to which we can travel and feel relaxed, comfortable and content. Most often these are places we've been to, where we have experienced the emotions of safety, security and comfort. Sometimes they are places we only dream of visiting, yet are confident our experience will be one of comfort and peace. It is important to allow oneself the benefit of time to travel to these places of comfort and security when in need. They are an invaluable part of one's personal support system.

At times, even the most familiar places are anything but comfortable. Our home, our workplace, and even our regular places of relaxation (the tennis court, the health club, the golf course, the library, the park) can all become old, or routine. We need to be able to give ourselves permission to physically remove ourselves from these familiar old haunts and travel to a special place where we know we can find comfort. We know that with that comfort and security comes a sense of renewal. These places are not places in which one finds isolation or casual diversions which tend to separate us from the inner connectedness of life. Rather, these places are sources of perspective whereby one can establish that sense of renewal and reinvigoration, and become ready to reenter one's life. Life will still be filled with the daily stresses, trials, challenges, and successes, but one's coping mechanisms will be activated with renewed vigor.

A special place in your personal support system need not be a little inn on the *Champs Elysees* in Paris, or a native hut on a pristine beach in Bora Bora. Obviously we all have budgetary constraints, and even our place of personal renewal must be within our means. It may be a cabin in the mountains or at the lake; it may be a motel by the beach, or a campground in the desert. Our place doesn't have to be famous or fancy; it only has to afford us the calming sense of replenishment we seek.

The second and perhaps the most important component of our personal support system is the human component. Very few of us maintain a completely isolated existence. Some try, for a little while or a long time, but most eventually find a distinct need for human interaction. Both as children and adults, we do need to belong to a group, or several groups. There are many ways we may establish the criteria for the group or groups we choose to be a member of. For some, a primary support group might be family. For others, a support group may consist of selected friends, co-workers, along with an intimate partner. The essential ingredient in the selection of human membership for your personal support system lies in the element of choice. Too many of us accept the family member who lives closest, or the co-worker who has the work station next to ours, as members of our support group. Often the people who are thrown together by circumstance make wonderful members of your support group. But this is not always the case.

There is no need to accept members of your support group simply due to geographic proximity or familial relationship. The choice must be free and open; it's all solely up to you. Choices made out of desperation, loneliness and isolation tend to lead to counterproductive support systems. When we find ourselves lonely and desperate for company, we often assume that being with *anyone* is preferable to being alone. This is seldom true. It is clearly much better to be at home alone trimming your toenails than to be out "having fun" with people who aren't positive influences. We cannot accept attention that is largely negative without it having a significant negative effect on our self-esteem.

Often individuals seek to involve themselves in your support system in order to fulfill needs of their own which may be incompatible with yours. Often, too, people feel a need to behave negatively toward others in order to feel better about themselves. These people can severely sabotage your efforts, like the overweight person who is always offering tempting goodies when you're trying to diet. Being the recipient of such behavior or such an attitude yields nothing except an assault on your self-concept.

We must allow ourselves complete freedom in building our own support system to our own standards and ideals. You may find certain members of your family counterproductive to your sense of growth and health. This does not mean you are being disloyal or unloving to your family.

Despite the fact that they're part of your immediate family, these individuals do not belong in your personal support group, and you must not allow any rationalization, internal or external, to alter that fact.

Along with one or more family members who provide positive, supportive input, you may choose friends, colleagues, neighbors, anyone you feel good about and communicate well with, to form your personal support system. Over time, with direction and conscientious effort, this group becomes tightly knit, reliable, and comforting. But it is not a one-way street. In order to develop and maintain the human element of your personal support system, you need to nurture your support group members in return. Just as "To have a friend, you must be a friend," you will need to be able to ask for their help and support, and you'll need to be able to give them help and support as well.

Sometimes, in crisis, you need to ask for members of your support group to listen, and perhaps provide guidance and advice. At other times you just need a friendly ear to share conversations and good times. Don't share just the bad times or rough times with your support group. Learn to share the joys as well, for while they can share in sorrow, why should they be deprived of sharing happiness? A support group is built upon mutual caring and trust. It is important for you to support and uplift members of your support group, and sharing good news is part of that.

The act of giving to members of your support group through listening and sharing support is not completely unselfish. You do not give to these people solely to receive their support in return. There is a biological term which applies here: *symbiosis.* It is defined as being together in a more or less intimate association which is mutually beneficial. By giving to members of your group, you gain positive input to your own self-concept. Being a good support group member is every bit as important to your self-esteem as having a good personal support system.

If you have an intimate partner with whom you share your life, that partner should be a part of your support group. If your partner does not fit comfortably into your support group, that may serve as an indication that there is a need for change, either in the support group membership, the support membership standards, or in your relationship with your intimate partner.

It is important to note that not all elements of your personal support system will necessarily go together at the same time. Some elements of your support system will not even have an opportunity to meet. At times, traveling to a comfortable and safe place should be done with a member or two of your human personal support system; at other times, such travel should be done alone. At times, your relationship with a particular member of your personal support system may be an issue of concern for you. When that is the case, the other individual member or members of your support system that you choose to discuss the issue with must be carefully selected. Any utilization of your personal support system must be guided by your own judgment. As in any and all human interrelationships, you must be aware of the many subtleties of personalities and other basic human characteristics, and consider them carefully and lovingly.

Emotional support is important. Emotional support may be given through an empathetic ear, a pat on the back, a smile. In any truly empathetic relationship, a degree of objectivity is essential. Members of your personal support system must be free to provide the support required without personal bias that comes from being too highly involved with the issue at hand. By paying careful attention to the issue of objectivity, without sacrificing the human caring so essential, one chooses the best elements of one's personal support system for any given situation.

The **Third Key** to strong personal values and positive self-esteem is: **Develop and maintain a strong personal**

support system.   As John Donne said, "No man is an island." It was true in the seventeenth century; it's perhaps even more meaningful today. People need people.

We've defined what a personal support system is, and how to develop one for ourselves. We know who to call in times of need, but when those times arise, we say, "I can't bother John, or Betty . . . it's ten o'clock at night." Or, "he's probably watching the game," or "she's tired; I'd better call tomorrow." Many people find it very difficult to access their personal support system.

Helping others—lending support—is a positive experience.   In fact, it is a prime human experience. It helps both the giver and the recipient feel better and stronger and more fulfilled.

When you need a little feedback, or when you're in a major personal crisis, why shouldn't you contact your supporter?   Remember, you'll be giving that person the opportunity to feel good about themselves. Seeking support is an important adjunct to maintaining self-esteem. Providing support, similar to the twelfth step in Twelve Step Programs, affords us the opportunity to feel good about ourselves. Just offering help is self-helpful!

We see more and more clearly that the development of one's self-esteem is based on many issues, and utilizes input from a wide variety of sources. One of the key influences for one's self-image is how we view the achievement of our goals.

We Need to Set Realistic Goals

As we are constantly measuring our performance, it is important to accept some failures, and perhaps more important to achieve successes.

As with most issues, planning is an important part of goal-setting. You may be familiar with the adage "We rarely plan to fail; we simply fail to plan." It is true that we seldom plan for failure. Most often we fail because we neglected the planning process.

The **Fourth Key: Set realistic goals.** Accepting the importance of planning in setting goals and achieving success, we must emphasize that our planning must be realistic.

In order to set realistic goals, one needs to ensure that the goal is specific. The goal must be articulated to oneself in direct and understandable terms. The goal must be clear enough to enable us to direct our focus and energies toward successful attainment of the goal.

For example, if one wishes to lose weight, one is much more likely to be successful if a realistic amount of weight is specified as the goal, rather than simply saying, "Well, I guess I'd better lose some weight."

In one's effort to make the goal specific, it is important to make the goal feasible and reachable.

Many goals are just too big or grandiose for human achievement. Some goals may be reachable for others, but are unrealistic expectations for ourselves. Some are unrealistic due to exaggerated notions; some are unrealistic because they're just too darn big.

In our efforts to make our goals attainable, we need to consider our **realistic self-inventory** (the first Key in our process), and apply our strengths to the goal articulated. We need to then determine whether or not the goal is set realistically and in a manner in which it will be reachable for us. Sometimes the goal will be too big to acheive in any realistic assessment.

At this point it becomes important to entertain the issue of sub-goals. Often, through breaking down a large goal into smaller and very specific sub-goals, one is able to successfully attain one's original, larger goal. Remember that a climb of Mt. Everest begins with one step.

Often the key to accomplishing a major success is to accomplish minor successes in succession. Consider the individual who feels a need to lose 35 pounds. Without an opportunity to feel some success along the way, motivation to stick with a diet long enough to lose 35 pounds is very, very difficult to maintain. One is therefore more successful in his or her effort to lose 35 pounds if he or she establishes a realistic set of sub-goals, such as 10 pounds, then another 10 pounds, then another 10 pounds, and then the last 5 pounds.

As you embark upon any goal it is important to write it down and tell someone. Writing the goal down helps you to make it specific and to assess just how reachable it is. Having written the goal, one can determine whether it is more effective to break the goal into sub-goals, and, if so, how those sub-goals should be set.

Writing down the goal also increases your commitment.

The importance of telling someone cannot be overstated. It is important to ground your efforts in such a way as to make your motivation resistant to distraction, fatigue and frustration.

How do you make your efforts as focused as possible? Sharing your intentions with someone is a very powerful mechanism. When you make a commitment to yourself, that is indeed important. When you are able to share that commitment with someone else, you do not share the responsibility, but you do achieve a sense of obligation and hopefully gain support for your effort.

"When you are able to share that commitment, you do not share the responsibility, but you do achieve a sense of obligation and hopefully gain support for your effort."

It is important to ensure that a sense of obligation is a motivational factor, not an inhibitor. No one wishes to announce his or her commitment to a goal to someone who will, should they not achieve success, turn on them with "Nyah nyah nyah, I knew you couldn't do it," or perhaps more adult words with the same power to sting and hurt. It is important, then, to choose your confidant carefully. It is recommended that you choose the most appropriate person from your personal support system in whom to confide. It may be more than one person, but at least tell someone.

It is also essential, in your effort to achieve your goals, to make the goals your own.

So often we set tasks for ourselves that we believe we "should" undertake. We decide to change jobs or quit smoking or go back to school because our friend, family or loved one wishes it, or because we believe that someone we care for considers it important.

Whether true or simply our assumption, if the motivation for our goal lies in pleasing someone else, it is nothing but an artificial motivation, and as such, very weak. Our motivation is subject to the influence of others when it begins as a goal directed by another or others.

If people close to you wish you to undertake a goal, particularly a "self-improvement" goal, then consider their input. Consider the source, as the saying goes. Decide whether that goal fits you. If it does, then build a goal-setting plan around it, enlist the support of those others, and go for it. Once the goal is your own, you have gained the probability of achievement. If the goal does not fit you, then it most definitely should be discarded. Whatever the goal addresses is not your problem, at least not one you choose to acknowledge at this time. It is the problem of the person who tried to assign it to you; let them solve it for themselves.

As much as possible, the plan needed to achieve your goal must be dependent solely upon you. There are already far too many things in life that we cannot control. Our effort to achieve our goal is pure folly if it is a consequence of relying on other people or things beyond our direct control.

For example, if one decided to get into shape by developing an exercise program, he or she would probably set an achievable goal, with interim sub-goals, and then go to it. If a part of the exercise plan were to go to the gym to work out, and the gym were four or five miles away, and there was no public transportation available, and if the person couldn't drive, that would create a problem. The person might ask a friend to chauffeur them on Tuesdays, Thursdays and Saturdays. Then the friend might assure the person that the transportation would be made available. However, involving another person in a plan like this creates too many additional and uncontrollable variables. It is enough that things will come up and the person will not be able to get to the gym some days, but by depending on another person to meet his or her goal, our well-intentioned person opens the door to an even greater lack of control in achieving his or her goal. Even the best-laid plans can go awry. Why invite problems which thwart the goal?

A sixth element in realistic goal setting is to make the goal measurable.

We make our goals measurable either through time, quality or quantity. For example, if our goal is to lose weight, we might say that we will lose 35 pounds in three months. In this way we utilize time to measure our success. Alternatively, we might use quantity as our measure, and in this example simply say that our goal is to lose 35 pounds, and the loss of that number of pounds becomes our mark for assessing success or failure, regardless of time involved to achieve the weight loss. We might choose to ignore the number of pounds involved in our weight loss efforts, and not establish a time either. We might choose to look at it as a quality issue. We might decide that our weight loss effort is grounded in an effort to "look good" (hopefully by our own assessment). We might further decide that looking good means fitting into a particular dress or outfit. When we can comfortably fit into the clothes selected, then we know we have achieved our goal.

The last stage in realistic goal setting is evaluation.

We must always evaluate efforts undertaken to achieve our goals. It is true that by establishing a measurable goal, we can make our evaluation on a very clear, direct basis.

". . . any evaluation scheme must allow for shades of gray, or degrees of success and failure."

The evaluation step in this plan consists more of assessing the *degree* of success. We may have established 35 pounds as our goal, and we may have only lost 30 pounds. Does this mean we have failed? We are our own judge and jury.

Failure and success are seldom black and white issues. While we need clarity in order to understand our goals, plan our efforts, and assess our degree of success, any evaluation scheme must allow for shades of gray, or degrees of success and failure. We constantly utilize our Performance Ratio, applying it to all our behaviors, attitudes, and even to thoughts, to evaluate the degree of appropriateness. Often the application of that Performance Ratio is counterproductive, yielding negative input to our self-concept. Most often the difference between success and failure lies in the degree of success we have gained in our behavior. At times failure or success is dependent upon poorly defined goals and poorly defined plans to achieve those goals. Through the utilization of an effective and realistic goal setting program, we minimize the chances of judging our performance inappropriately. Our judgment will rest much more on our actual performance and its merits than on our planning ability.

Checklist for Seven Steps to Goal-Setting

1. Make the goal specific.
2. Make the goal reasonable and reachable.
3. Plan specific sub-goals.
4. Write the goal down, and tell it to a trusted

someone.
5. Be sure the g oal is your own, not someone else's idea of what you should do.
6. Make the goal measurable.
7. Establish evaluation criteria in advance.

We Must Be Assertive

We also need to understand the importance of being assertive, and undertake assertive behavior in all aspects of our life. Our **Fifth Key** to strong personal values and positive self-esteem: **Be assertive**.

Assertiveness means standing up for what you believe in, for what you believe is right, and taking control to assure the desired results are gained. Assertiveness also means taking into account the needs, feelings and thoughts of others.

If one goes out to get everything he or she feels entitled to without any regard to the needs and interests of others, such an attitude tends to lead to aggressive behavior. We've all seen the movies in which the "bad guy" simply mows down any opposition to his acheivement of his goals, however misguided. There is no reason to believe that your needs are more important than the needs of your family, friends and neighbors.

On the other side of the coin, in our society there is a tendency to deny our needs. Often this denial is based in fear. We are unsure as to the outcome of our efforts if we try to go after what we believe in; moreover, we are reluctant to face failure. So, if there is a chance we will fail to get what we want or need, too often we don't try. We delude ourselves into thinking that if we do not try, then we eliminate the possibility of failure.

The flaw in this thinking is found in the fact that choosing to not try is indeed a choice in itself. By choosing to not try, we do not guard against failure; rather, we guarantee it.

If there is something we believe we deserve, and we choose not to ask for it, then there is no way, with the possible exception of divine intervention or blind luck, we can obtain it, whatever it may be.

Any time we choose, usually out of fear, to not go after what we believe we deserve, we give ourselves an incredibly powerful message. We tell ourselves we are not worth what we really believe we are worth.

Your mother, your employer, and your friend can each tell you that you just aren't worth anything. If you have figured out that you are worth something, but do not ask for it, then you are telling yourself in a much more powerful and potent way that they were right—that you do not deserve what you believe you're worth. If that is the message you transmit to yourself, then that is the message you receive. Such a message has a devastating effect on your self-concept.

If you truly believe that you deserve a raise at your place of employment, then you need to ask yourself, does your supervisor or the group of people who have the power to raise your salary know that you believe you deserve a raise? If the answer is no, then you most likely have only yourself to blame for not getting a raise.

A word of caution: If you work for a person or a group of people who would fire you or cause you great discomfort if you asked about a raise, or let them know you believe you deserve one, then you should not bring up the subject of a raise with that person or group. It is a sad reality that there are unfair situations like this; nevertheless, it's important that you remember this is where your strategic judgment comes in.

No one is suggesting that you should deny reality in being assertive. One would have to consider the possibility of changing jobs in order to get out of a situation that precludes the opportunity to be assertive. In such a case, beginning a job search would be the assertive thing to do.

Being assertive and expressing your own rightful needs is so terribly important.

If you express your belief that you deserve a raise, and do not get one, then again it is your choice as to whether to stay, or to start looking for another job and quit upon finding one. The issue is not in getting everything you need or feel you deserve; rather, the issue is being able to express your needs in an appropriate manner.

In an appropriate manner is the key element here. One could easily stand up and say, "I need this, I want this, I must have it, and I will have it." This is seldom appropriate.

We've established that "no man is an island." We note, too, that one's needs are seldom completely independent of the needs and wishes and rights of others. Any denial of self-assertiveness is self-destructive. But any effort to be assertive while denying the needs and rights of others yields only aggressive behavior, which in turn invariably leads to counterproductive situations. People who are aggressive do not tend to get what they're after; rather, they tend to promote defensiveness in other people. They appear to be selfish, and the responses of others to that selfishness yield once again a negative blow to the aggressor's self-concept.

The concept of concern for the consequences of one's actions in relation to other people is known as social responsibility. Being socially responsible is being accountable for oneself and one's actions, and acting responsibly toward others. There can be no positive self-esteem for a person who disregards social responsibility.

Even if relatively passively, society reinforces the importance

"Being socially responsible is being accountable for oneself and one's actions, and to act responsibly toward others. There can be no positive self-esteem for a person who disregards social responsibility."

of self-esteem. When our social interaction is non-productive, non-satisfying or hurtful, we take at least some portion of hurt upon ourselves. When we offer social support, we feel self-satisfied and often justifiably proud. Behaving as a responsible member of society and generally "contributing to the common good" enhances self-esteem.

To Err is Human; to Forgive Necessary

Our **Sixth Key** toward developing and maintaining a positive sense of self-esteem: **Accept the humanness of yourself and others.**

What does it mean to accept humanness?

Consider the cliché "To err is human, to forgive divine." To err is indeed human; forgiveness must also become a human skill.

All our lives, we grow up hearing, "You must learn from your mistakes." This is a viable and admirable concept. We all make mistakes. We made mistakes yesterday. We made mistakes today, and we will make mistakes tomorrow. It is important to learn from mistakes, and hopefully to not make the same mistakes again.

As human beings, we have a tendency to concentrate on the mistakes we've made. If asked to consider our personal histories, and write all the significant events to which we have contributed in our lives, it is my contention that our list of mistakes will be much, much longer than our list of successes.

Is this because we have truly made more mistakes that we have achieved successes? On the contrary. We are constantly bombarded with messages that suggest we need to focus on our mistakes to ensure that we don't make them again, to ensure that we indeed learned from them, and on and on.

At this same time we are inundated with messages that say "Don't stress your accomplishments," and "It's not polite to brag." To do so is to appear selfish, conceited and egocentric. We do not want to appear selfish, conceited and egocentric; nor do we want to appear difficult to get along with. We do not want others to appear difficult, either.

Any effort to promote oneself is generally met with accusations of arrogance or an inflated sense of self-importance and grandiosity. No one is suggesting that pompous attitudes and behavior are good things. Arrogance is definitely undesirable, and should be discouraged. But it may be a matter of perception.

It is my belief that most arrogant people are not arrogant at all. Most people who seem arrogant are actually insecure, using the mask of arrogance to conceal their true selves from the public and from themselves. Their efforts to convince others as well as themselves that they are adept, skillful, and worthwhile human beings are often based on insincere and irrational beliefs. For them the cover of arrogance is a necessary camouflage.

"Along with the acceptance that humans make mistakes must come the element of forgiveness—of others, and of self."

A balance must be achieved between low self-esteem and arrogance. Such a balance is achievable, basically through honest, sincere and well-founded self-acceptance.

Self-acceptance stems from a realistic self-inventory, an effort to be true to one's values, maintenance and development of a support system, realistic goals, and an effort to maintain constructively assertive behavior, all tied together with a forgiving view of mistakes.

Along with the acceptance that humans make mistakes must come the element of forgiveness—forgiveness of others, and forgiveness of self.

If we fail to forgive others, we tend to carry resentment, anger and other emotions that are counterproductive to accepting ourselves. Few of us wish to be the person who carries resentment and anger. The insidious fact of resentment is that it eats away at the person who feels it, while never even being noticed or acknowledged by the person who spawned it

Even so, it is often easier to work on forgiving others than it is to forgive ourselves.

The concept that forgiveness is only the providence of God—as in ". . . to forgive [is] divine"—is nonproductive. Religion teaches us that God forgives sins, and in that context that is appropriate. But when it comes to the issue of our own behavior, if it would be considered not in our power to forgive, we would only carry grudges. Grudges against others lead to resentments, as noted above, and grudges against ourselves serve as cracks in any foundation we try to develop for a positive self-concept. These cracks grow into chasms, and over time destroy any hope we might have for self-acceptance and growth.

Self-acceptance is the key to growth. Self-acceptance is born out of self-awareness, and self-forgiveness. Self-forgiveness is achieved through an initial understanding of one's place in the scheme of things.

We as humans are an immeasurably important element in this world. We are thinking, feeling beings. We are elements of growth and catalysts for change. Most of us are constantly striving for progress and success. There is nothing wrong with this effort, unless it traps us into the inability to forgive ourselves when we stray from our path.

Only perfection could prevent the possibility of failure in any given human endeavor. Perfection is a concept perhaps best left in the heavens. Perhaps God is perfect; we know humans are not. So, if we accept that we are less than perfect, then we must accept the fact of mistakes. If we truly accept mistakes as part of life, then we must offer forgiveness if we are to progress.

It strikes me as odd that as we grow and develop into

fully functioning adult human beings, we tend to gain a perspective that enables us to forgive the errors of others. We forgive our friends as they often fall short of our expectations and hopes; we forgive our children as their behavior disappoints us. We say that they made a mistake, but we love them. We get over it and move along.

How often do we say to ourselves, "I made a mistake but I still love me"? Not very often.

We are our own worst critics. What we accept and forgive in others we find so terribly hard to accept and forgive in ourselves. We allow others to make mistakes; we do not allow the same for ourselves.

When we make little mistakes, such as forgetting to pick up our dry cleaning, or being late for an appointment, do we acknowledge the error and embark on a course of forgiveness? No. What we most often do is, we berate ourselves. We say to ourselves, and occasionally to others, "How can I be so stupid? I forgot the dry cleaning!" "I was half an hour late! They must think I'm an idiot!"

While our main point might indeed be our concern over our failure to remember the dry cleaning, or our failure to allow sufficient travel time, we hurt ourselves with negative behavioral accusations instead of building and bettering ourselves with self-acceptance and forgiveness. Just as the parent has the power to hamper the child by dwelling on the failures and refusing forgiveness, so we hamper our own self-image by doing the same.

This taunting ourselves with our mistakes and failures is called negative self-talk. (How dumb can I be?; I'm so forgetful; I'm so stupid; I always screw up; Will I never learn? I must be totally worthless.) It is a form of self-punishment. We don't utilize negative self-talk as penance or repentance, achieving forgiveness through being nasty to ourselves. We simply berate ourselves. We belittle ourselves. We may think it helpful to point our our errors in this way, but instead of being helpful, we punish ourselves for being human.

The use of positive affirmations has proven to be effective to counteract the effects of negative self-talk over the years, once the negative self-talk is stopped. Self-empowerment programs have utilized "happy homework statements" and additional positive affirmations, ranging from "I am a good person" to the universal affirmation "Every day in every way I'm getting better and better." [Interestingly, this affirmation is attributed to Emile Coué (1857-1926). It was the formula of his faith cures, inscribed in his sanitorium in Nancy, France.] By consistently applying positive messages, the self gains strength. Our self gains independence and a sense of identity based on our belief in our strengths and our accomplishments, and our forgiveness for our mistakes. This is indeed how true acceptance of our humanness works.

Due to the pressures of our society, it is often difficult to forgive our mistakes. There is a tendency toward demanding perfection even while acknowledging that it is unattainable. This self-defeating, convoluted thinking is crazy-making. It may be the root of the issue of co-dependence. It is certainly the root of much maladaptive behavior, as it is born out of the desire to reach for something we know we cannot have. At its very simplest, it is an example of unrealistic goal setting.

In an effort to combat this reaching for the unattainable, one might apply the concept of time and space to one's behavior. Most mistakes are unintentional. Our behavior is undertaken based on the best information we have at any given time, and the best intentions we have at that time. Most behaviors are identified as mistakes only in hindsight. The identification comes after new information has been presented, or at the very least, the circumstances that we endeavored to predict turned out to be something other than what we had hoped or expected. Hindsight reveals we have made mistakes. Of course, if we knew then what we know now, we wouldn't have made the mistakes! So why, with that knowledge, are we left with such difficulty in our efforts to achieve forgiveness and self-acceptance?

True, sometimes we have the information before us, we assess it accurately, and still decide to undertake behavior that is likely to prove harmful and mistaken. In these cases, we need to maintain a sense of forgiveness and understand that we sometimes make bad choices and that's okay. We need to learn from that. In fact, we need to build upon it, and go on from there.

The first stage in successfully dealing with the knowledge that one has made a mistake is, one needs to identify who is calling the behavior mistaken? Who is the critic? Does the critic have a good point? Regardless of whether the critic is a friend, a colleague, a supervisor or a teacher, they may be accurate, or they may be inaccurate. Your second goal after identifying the critic is to give an honest appraisal as to the degree of their accuracy.

If you determine that the critic is inaccurate, then you need to assertively report back to the critic that they were wrong, and perhaps thank them for their interest. This applies to critics other than yourself, and to your own criticism as well.

If, in your honest appraisal, it is your determination that the criticism has accuracy, then you need to take it to heart, consider it, and decide what to do with the information. Perhaps you will set realistic goals and make some changes in order to accomodate that criticism and use it for growth.

A key element in dealing with criticism lies in applying one's sense of judgment honestly and appropriately to the criticism, and deciding upon its accuracy and relevance. I believe that an even more important element necessary to successfully deal with criticism lies in one's ability to act upon the criticism without blowing it out of proportion, or dwelling on it.

So many times after we accept a criticism and act upon

it as being appropriate, or reject it as being inappropriate, we continue to dwell on the criticism. We chew on it, stew over it, and allow it to become magnified and uncontrollable. So the criticism rears its ugly head and assaults our personhood.

Once again, this has to do with forgiveness. It is our inability, or our apparent inability, to achieve self-forgiveness that enables us to dwell on criticism.

We Need to Pat Ourselves on the Back

What's important, when it is all said and done, is to see the *positive* aspects of mistakes and criticism. We must accept criticism, just as we accept mistakes, and turn them into tools by evaluating the input they afford us, learning from that input, making changes as appropriate, and moving on.

The **Seventh Key** to strong personal values and positive self-esteem lies in what could be viewed as the fullest extension of accepting and building on criticism and mistakes: **Take a moment for self-praise.**

While taking some time out to say, "Good job," or "You did that really well!" may sound conceited or arrogant, it is far from it. In fact, self-praise is essential to recognizing your strengths and maintaining your motivation. When self-praise is based on an honest assessment of your behavior or performance, then it is nothing but a genuine and deserved response. A little praise for yourself whenever it is merited, for successes large and small, provides a solid foundation and building blocks for growth.

Just as it is important to share our goals, and to seek support and assistance with issues of self-doubt from members of our personal support system, it is equally important to share with them our self-praise. There is really no risk of accusations of arrogance, because you have nurtured the relationship and developed the trust to ensure such shared self-praise is properly received and acknowledged.

It is most important to hear yourself praise yourself, but the added benefit of having someone else share your self-praise provides an extra boost to your positive sense of self. Once again, it is important to share with a trusted person. It is overwhelmingly true that by taking someone else into your self-praise, you're taking an important step toward fully acknowledging your self-worth, and making it an accepted reality.

The Seven Keys to Strong Personal Values and Positive Self-Esteem

1. Establish and maintain a realistic **personal self-inventory**;

2. Be true to your **values**;

3. Identify and develop your **support system**;

4. Set realistic **goals**;

5. Be **assertive**;

6. Fully accept your humanness (**forgive**), and

7. Take a moment for **self-praise**.

These key elements to the establishment and maintenance of strong personal values and positive self-esteem are not exclusive step-by-step points. There is no sequential order they fall into. One must establish a working relationship with these keys, adapt them to his or her individual lifestyle, and adopt them as tools to work with through life.

There is no time like right now to begin working on your self-inventory, understanding and developing your values, identifying and developing your support system, setting realistic goals, being assertive, fully accepting your human-ness, and taking a moment for self-praise. Indeed, all of the seven Keys are within your grasp, right now.

Begin now. Do it now.

The process is a living process. It begins at this moment, and it goes on throughout your life.

The Keys are in your hands. Stay with these Keys to stong values and positive self-esteem, and you will provide for yourself:

Nourishment

Acceptance

A foundation for growth.

Your reward will be a strong sense of personal satisfaction, fulfillment and contentment, an honorable acknowledgment of your personal responsibility, and a validation that you are a productive asset to the community as a viable and valuable human being.

Enjoy your selfhood. Full esteem ahead!

EPILOGUE

Here you are, at the end of a personal-develpement book, addressing your new beginning. And you are ready. You've got the tools:

You're ready to list and maintain awareness of your strengths and limitations.

You've clarified your values, and you're committed to sticking to them.

You know your support system, and you're prepared to nurture it.

You know that your needs count, and you're determined to be direct and up-front with those needs.

You know you're human, and you know that you can and will make mistakes. But you also know mistakes are learning tools and can be forgiven. So you know how to forgive yourself as well as others.

And, wonderfully, you can accept self-praise for your acheivements, and even just for taking risks, win or lose, because you know it's justified.

Sounds like you've been given license to be terribly selfish, but you know better. You know that this book has given you the power of personal responsibility and confidence—of strong personal values and positive self-esteem.

A vital concept you've gained is that you are not alone in your own private world. We are all part of a very large world, the precious, irreplaceable environment which we all share with each other. That means your strengths and limitations, though they are your very own, must be considered in the greater context of humanity: in relation to your family, friends and those around you, and on the broader scope of the world society.

Your support system works largely by building and nurturing relationships with others. So you respect the needs of others as you do your own. You forgive others as you forgive yourself. You recognize the efforts and successes of others as you recognize those of your own.

Even your basic core values exist in the context of the elements of your shared world. Selfish values are irresponsible. Values which are responsible are those which allow for diversity of thought, opinion, and preference. Responsible values enable you to have the flexibility essential to meet the challenges of conflict and change.

Socially responsible values—those that temper our needs and desires with a responsiveness to the needs and wishes of others—offer the ticket to full personal responsibility. There is no self-esteem without personal responsibility; there is no personal responsibility without balance. And it is the balance afforded by personal responsibility that allows for the building of self-esteem.

It's very easy to abuse the seven keys to strong personal values and positive self esteem in which this book culminates. There may always be the temptation to take those keys to the extreme, in order to justify arrogance and selfishness. If winning and getting your way at any cost is your goal, you can certainly accomplish that. But you will do so at significant cost: you will not walk away with a sense of pride and self-fulfillment. Guaranteed.

Know that *balance*—an awareness and acceptance of our interconnectedness to our human environment, and an equal emphasis and nurturing to both that environment and ourselves—unfailingly leads to self-fulfillment.

Balance stokes the coals and provides the energy for unending self-improvement.

Know balance. Feel balance. Trust it. Honor it.

You're ready. You're on your way.

Full esteem ahead!

APPENDICES

STRENGTH BOMBARDMENT EXERCISE

STEP 1   Grab a pen and several sheets of paper,
         and a watch, clock or timer.

STEP 2   Find a quiet place; make yourself
         comfortable.

STEP 3   Consider the last week, and think
         over everything you said or did that
         you feel *good* about.

STEP 4   Set the clock for five (5) minutes;
         GO!
         Write down all the things you've reflected
         on in Step 3.

more...

STEP 5   After five minutes, STOP.

STEP 6   Ask yourself these questions:

                Did anything I wrote
                surprise me?

                How did it feel to go
                through this exercise?

                The STRENGTH BOMBARDMENT
                EXERCISE simply gives you
                permission to acknowledge the
                power inside you, and the good
                you're already doing.

                Repeat as needed.

BIBLIOGRAPHY

Brooks, B. David and Dalby, Rex, *The Self-Esteem Repair and Maintenance Manual*. REDA Press, Long Beach, CA; 1992.

Browne, Harry, *How I Found Freedom in an Unfree World*. MacMillan Publishing, New York NY; 1973.

Chaney, Casey, *Pardon My Dust . . . I'm Remodeling*. Mocha Publishing, Beaverton OR; 1990.

Coopersmith, Stanley, *The Antecedents of Self-Esteem*. W.H. Freeman, San Francisco CA; 1967.

Dauw, Dean, *Increasing Your Self-Esteem*. Waveland Press Inc., Prospect Heights OR; 1980.

Jeffers, Susan, *Feel the Fear and Do It Anyway*. Fawcett Columbine, New York NY; 1987.

more...

Johnson, Helen, *How Do I Love Me?* (Second Edition). Sheffield Publishing Company, Salem OR; 1986.

McKay, Matthew and Fanning, Patrick, *Self-Esteem.* New Haringer Publications, Oakland CA; 1988.

Peele, Stanton, *How Much is Too Much.* Prentice-Hall, Inc., Englewood Cliffs NJ; 1981.

Satir, Virginia, *Peoplemaking.* Science Behavior Books, Palo Alto, CA; 1972.

Simon, Sidney, *Vultures.* Argus Communications, Allen, TX; 1977.

Silverstein, Lee, *Consider the Alternative.* Compcare Publications, Minneapolis, MN; 1980.

Simmermacher, Donald, *Self-Image Modification.* Health Communications, Inc., Deerfield Beach FL; 1989.

ABOUT THE AUTHOR

Rob Solomon was born in Winnipeg, Canada, where he received his undergraduate degree in Psychology and worked as a counselor in a chemical dependency treatment program. After graduating from the University of North Dakota with a Master of Arts degree in Counseling, Mr. Solomon continued his work in counseling in the American Midwest.

In 1983, Mr. Solomon relocated to the Pacific Northwest, where he directed a chemical dependency treatment and education program. After six years of clinical supervision and program management, he began to devote full-time to private practice.

As a Licensed Professional Counselor, Rob Solomon sees clients and devotes considerable time to presenting workshops and training programs for various groups. He retains faculty status at several colleges in the Pacific Northwest.

Rob Solomon Consulting is based in Beaverton, Oregon, where Mr. Solomon lives with his wife and two children.